Astounding Truths of the Bible

A Bite-Sized Approach to Understanding the World's Bestselling Book

ANNIE WEBER

Published by hope*books
2217 Matthews Township Pkwy
Suite D302
Matthews, NC 28105
www.hopebooks.com
hope*books is a division of hope*media

Printed in the United States of America by hope*books

First paperback edition.
ISBN: 979-8-89185-004-0 (Paperback)
ISBN: 979-8-89185-013-2 (Hardcover)
ISBN: 979-8-89185-005-7 (Ebook)
Library of Congress Number: 2023916123

hope*books
hopebooks.com

This book is dedicated to my husband, Bryan D. Weber. No other person has been as instrumental in challenging me to seek Truth. Also, no other person has served as my personal sanctification aid, allowing me to grow closer to Christ through the experiences we have had in our marriage. I am so thankful to God for the opportunity He has given me to be your wife.

To my kids—Lucy, Luke, Lily, and Levi—this was written for you. It was written around you. It was written in the car during volleyball and basketball practices. It was written while you napped. It was written while you played and while I let you binge watch TV so I could write (you're welcome).

And most importantly, this book is dedicated to the Lord. Writing about God is my favorite form of worship.

CONTENTS

Part II—God's Desire for His People

Part III—Curious Parts of the Bible

Part IV—God Equips His People

PREFACE

I never opened a Bible until I was twenty-eight years old. Until that point, I was chasing my fleshly desires and was fully convinced the world revolved around me. However, by God's grace, Jesus stepped into my identity struggles and the Gospel of Christ became personal.

At that time, I traded my animal-print heels and working woman duds for more casual garments that accommodated my new life as a full-time homemaker. Highly influenced by the world, I had a keen awareness that success was measured by title, status, paycheck, and pursuit of self. However, God met me in our tiny apartment in Manhattan, (the Little Apple, not the Big Apple) Kansas, because I chose to open the Bible and quietly read, study, and learn while my baby, Lucy, slept soundly for hours every day. Lucy exited the womb and cut her own umbilical cord. She has been independent since birth, so when she determined that her daily dual nap schedule would be as consistent as the rising sun, I was thankful that my daily study time in the Word was equally as consistent.

During that season of transition, in addition to my career path being redirected, my understanding of the faith adapted. I began to know God in a personal way. Never mind the heavy hitters of the faith like Billy Graham and R.C. Sproul, my awakening was so intense, I felt like I was the world's first theologian. I read the Bible with such shock and awe. I could not believe that the Bible provided so much incredible instruction for life and God's character was so aptly described through the words of Scripture.

I have no theology degree, nor am I an academic. These Astounding Truths were written to assist the reader in understanding the timelessness of God's Word, with a twenty-first century perception. My hope is that by reading *Astounding Truths of the Bible*, your desire to know God and His Word is magnified. I offer no assistance for the reader who is struggling between denominations. This collection of 100 Astounding Truths is only to promote the Bible. You will find many more talented authors who can eloquently engage in theological debates, but the book you hold in your hands is inspired by my own love of diving deeper into Scripture and understanding the words of God more thoroughly. Whether you cut your teeth on the Bible, or have never opened a Bible, it is not by accident that you are holding this book now.

My desire is that by reading these Astounding Truths, you gain a healthy awareness of the vast differences between living in the world and living for the Lord. The Bible uses two words (salt and light) to describe the response that followers of Christ should have when exposed to the precepts of the faith. My hope is that this book will help you understand how to be salty in a decaying culture and how to be a light in a dark world. I don't expect you to have an encounter with Jesus, I expect you to be *transformed* by Him.

Each Astounding Truth ends in a **bold** prayer. The prayer serves as a model of how a Christ follower can pray, according to the respective passage of Scripture. I challenge you to join me in praying boldly regarding these Truths, and let the Holy Spirit speak to you about how you can grow in your prayer life as you pray the scriptures.

The first twenty-five Astounding Truths are centered around the character of God. We'll weave back and forth throughout the Old and New Testaments in this section to gain insights into who God is. By getting to know Him, you will more thoroughly understand His character and develop a better appreciation for His attributes. When we have a solid understanding of the dynamic character of God, our worship is enhanced. The Bible is the fundamental way we learn about the character of God. Congratulations, and welcome to the Astounding Truths of the Bible. Thank you for joining me on this journey!

PART I

The Character of God

-›››››‹‹‹‹-

God Sees Differently

But the Lord said to Samuel, "Do not look at his appearance or at his physical stature, because I have refused him. For the Lord does not see as man sees; for man looks at the outward appearance, but the Lord looks at the heart."

—1 SAMUEL 16:7

S ometimes my family of six will walk through nature in nice-ish, color coordinated clothes. Our family Christmas card photo is annual proof. Other times, we roll out of bed and trudge through the day looking like unkempt swamp monsters.

We invest so much time and money in our outward appearances. However, the Bible presents a message about our appearance that is contrary to the world's response. No matter how hard I strive to get everyone looking like we belong on the next cover of *Focus on the Family Magazine*, God cares more about our hearts than how polished we look in our photo shoot. The Bible reveals God's character by revealing how He sees. He "does not see as man sees." His vision is contrary to our vision. We learn in 1 Samuel about how God has a significantly different view of our appearance than we have.

Knowing the circumstances that triggered this conversation between God and Samuel is important in order to understand this text in 1 Samuel 16. The chapter is titled "David Anointed King," and opens with Samuel moping over the loss of King Saul. The Bible tells us that an altercation occurred between wicked King Saul and Samuel in the previous chapter. In an angry rage, Saul tore Samuel's robe (1 Sam. 15:27). God uses that clothing snafu as a model for what the king had coming. Just as King Saul tore Samuel's robe, God would tear the kingdom away from Saul.

With Saul terminated from his kingly duties, God's people found themselves without a leader. The Lord sent Samuel to Bethlehem to find a replacement. God made it clear that he had chosen one of Jesse's eight sons to be the next king. When Samuel saw the oldest son, he expected the good-looking guy standing before him to be the best fit for the open position as king. But God, in His infinite wisdom, had a different plan. One by one, each of the sons were brought out. All of them were strong, handsome, and perfectly qualified, according to human understanding. However, none of them were God's choice for the next king over Israel. David was the one God intended to lead His people because he remained close to God in his early life.

At 30 years old, God called David out of his shepherding career and transitioned him into his role as king over God's people (2 Sam. 5:4). This testimony teaches us that humans can tell how people *look*, but God can tell who they *are*. According to God, Jesse's youngest son, David, was the most qualified because of his lifelong faithfulness to God, his repentant heart, and his unwavering love for God. He was an unlikely choice as far as Jesse could tell, but God does not favor people according to how the world favors people. Sometimes He honors and blesses people who have not been regarded by others, as we see in the case of David. His heart was seen by God, and God rewarded this young shepherd boy for his faithfulness and used his life as a powerful testimony to how a man lives the highs and lows of a life in faithful service to God.

Lord, Open the eyes of my heart and allow me the opportunity to see people as You see them. Help me to be drawn to people for the Godly and quality character traits they possess. I heed this warning to not rely on the outward appearances of people, knowing that the heart can be deceitful. Bless me with wisdom to see the heart of others as You see them. Amen.

-»»»«««-

God Provides Unexpected Meetings

*Jesus answered and said to her, "Whoever drinks of this water will
thirst again, but whoever drinks of the water that I shall give him will
never thirst. But the water that I shall give him will become in him a
fountain of water springing up into everlasting life."*

—*JOHN 4:13–14*

Wintertime was approaching in West Michigan. As I walked through
campus, my apprehension toward cold weather bloomed. I found
myself daydreaming about warmer weather more than fantasizing about passing
my classes, so I pushed pause on my collegiate academic pursuits during my
sophomore year and moved to Florida to work at the *Polynesian Resort*. Living
in an entertainment capital like Orlando allowed me to have many unexpected
meetings with famous musicians and actors. Sometimes, the people you meet
unexpectedly have the biggest impact on your life.

This statement proves to be true in John 4. In this chapter we read a narrative
in which two people end up meeting unexpectedly while traveling—Jesus and a
woman. These two people have absolutely no business interacting with each other.
Social norms at the time of the encounter prohibited interaction for two reasons:
men were not allowed to engage in dialogue with women publicly, and the woman
was from a region where her ancestors had a reputation of being enemies with
God's people. This woman was a Samaritan. The relationship between God's
people and the Samaritan people can be summed up in one word: archenemies.

The hatred between Jews and Samaritans was fierce and long-standing, going all the way back to the days of the Patriarchs, then continuing through the division of the two kingdoms of Israel, and eventually to the time when Jesus walked the earth. For thousands of years, God's people despised Samaritans—that is why the story of the woman at the well is so profound and reveals God's character as "springs of living water."

Jesus entered this ongoing family feud and blew the proverbial hats off His travel companions in this text for a few reasons. First, He purposely journeyed to the region of Samaria to effect change, where previous religious leaders avoided it all together. Jesus came to earth to transform the lives of those following God *and* those who opposed any association with God. Jesus approached the Samaritan woman gathering water and requested a drink. The woman, having no idea she was speaking to the Messiah, was completely shocked by the fact that a sworn enemy would engage with her. She was puzzled by this unexpected meeting (just like I was baffled when I encountered Joey Fatone at a party during my season in Florida). Jesus responded by giving her a major clue as to who He was, but still left her to question who He might be.

Jesus used metaphorical language to explain Truth, the concept of "living water." The woman was still clueless, so Jesus again redirected the dialogue to get to the heart of who she was and what she wanted. The woman had a history of rejection by men and was alone (John 4:17). Without judging her relationship history, her five previous husbands, and current significant other who was not her husband, Jesus met her in her pain with mercy, and she realized who He was and why He came. She was so completely transformed by His character of "living water" that she went back to town and spoke with enthusiasm about her meeting with Jesus. This is the first record in Scripture of public evangelism, and it serves as encouragement to anyone who has suffered the pain of rejection.

Lord, while relationship pain is overwhelming, You are merciful to show compassion to people like the unnamed woman at the well. Like the woman, allow me to be transformed by Your living water. You are the Eternal God who restores our hearts and minds when we face rejection. Amen.

-))))))))))))-

God is the Original Matchmaker

Now Boaz said to her at mealtime, "Come here, and eat of the bread, and dip your piece of bread in the vinegar." So she sat beside the reapers, and he passed parched grain to her; and she ate and was satisfied, and kept some back.

—RUTH 2:14

My love story could have been written by Nicholas Sparks. Like his romance novels, the story of Bryan Weber and I began in North Carolina and incorporated elements of faith, family, friends, and patriotism. Sparks could not have written the tale any better than God sovereignly ordained our courtship. And just like his characters, during our courting we faced a hurdle that rewrote the plotline during a season of turmoil. This redirection triggered a solo reflective and growth season for each of us. During that time apart, we reassessed our priorities and career paths. After a season of sabbatical (every Sparks novel includes the devastating breakup), we transitioned back to a happily ever after romance, followed by a literal mountaintop marriage proposal in Colorado.

The entire Bible is a love story between God and His people. Through Scripture, we get glimpses of several love chronicles that provide models for how God outlines what a love story should (and should not) look like. In Ruth 2, we are introduced to Boaz, a man with a strange name and godly character traits. He falls in love with Ruth, while respecting her purity. He had her best interests at heart and did all he could do to ensure her safety. Boaz treated his servants well, honored God with his actions, and was very generous with his resources and wealth. Equally important, just like Bryan Weber, Boaz was generous in sharing his carbs with his girl on their first date (see Ruth 2:14 which quotes Boaz saying "Come here, and eat of the bread").

Understanding the love story of Ruth and Boaz allows us to get a glimpse of God's divine providence. God planted Ruth in the field owned by Boaz and His hand was upon her in a season of grief and trial. She was a young and childless widow. After her husband's death, she decided to remain in close proximity to her elderly mother-in-law to care for her, instead of returning to the land she came from (see Ruth 1:16). Since Ruth decided to remain with her mother-in-law Naomi, they found themselves relocating to Bethlehem and gleaning for food in a field owned by Boaz. The events leading up to the divine appointment between Boaz and Ruth reveal the redemptive character of God.

When God is the matchmaker, there are no mistakes in His work. Unlike match.com, eHarmony, and Tinder, when you let God do the work of the matchmaker, His perfect plan will be revealed. In the case of Boaz and Ruth, God brought them together to reveal His plan for all of humanity. Through this union, Ruth would experience the loving-kindness of both Boaz and the Lord. God eventually used this relationship in the lineage of Jesus (Matt. 1:5). We see that even though Ruth suffered pain and loss, God redeemed her tragedy into a beautiful story of hope and joy.

Lord, allow me the understanding of Your will regarding my relationships. Help me trust Your plan for my life and know that through my relationships You give me a glimpse of Your redemptive plan. Help me to model the character traits of Boaz and Ruth in my relationship. Amen.

->>>>?<<<<-

God is Sovereign Over Our Circumstances

And we know that all things work together for good to those who love
God, to those who are the called according to His purpose.

—ROMANS 8:28

When Carrie Underwood released a song in 2005 about Jesus taking the wheel, I did not exactly have Jesus in my life driving my Jeep. Jesus may have been in the backseat, perhaps entering through the hatchback on my best days, but more than likely he was running behind the vehicle as I sped away. The song which eventually made Billboard Hot Country Song #1 proclaimed a Biblically accurate and critical message to country music fans worldwide about the sovereignty of God. "Jesus Take the Wheel" is a poetic way of letting God ordain your path. It is complete recognition that the Lord is sovereign in all circumstances. It means trusting that He will drive your car, control the speed, navigate your GPS, and make pit stops as He sees fit.

Trusting God's sovereignty—supreme power and authority—means trusting that if the Lord has allowed something challenging, difficult, or shocking to happen, then He plans to use it mightily *if the person will let him.* Paul writes, "we know that in all things God works for the good of those who love him, who have been called according to his purpose." (Rom. 1:28) Paul is emphatically writing the message that the solution for understanding difficult times is about understanding life on God's terms. The "good" Paul is speaking of does not mean earthly comfort. Rather, it means aligning His people with His ways, bringing them into closer intimacy with Him, and inspiring a deeper awareness of the Lord working in the lives of His people.

God's sovereignty is knowing that He has ultimate control over E-V-E-R-Y-T-H-I-N-G and determines *all* outcomes, even when we may be uncomfortable. Some things will be ordained by God to refine us, mold our character, or turn us away from a sinful pattern. Nothing is out of the scope of the Lord's control, and nothing surprises Him. Although puzzling, aspects of the Lord's sovereignty are beyond our ability to understand on this side of Heaven. Our responsibility is to respond with obedience to what we understand about God and His love for all people.

Lord, allow me to remember that You guide my steps, according to Your perfect plan for my life. Help me to trust You when circumstances do not go according to my plan. Just as Carrie Underwood sings, ("I can't do this on my own") help me remember to rely on You for strength during seasons of trial. Amen.

-÷℈⟩⟩⟩℈⟨⟨⟨℈~

God Does Not Condone Excuses

And I said to them, 'Whoever has any gold, let them break it off.' So
they gave it to me, and I cast it into the fire, and this calf came out.
　　　　　　　　　　　　　　　　　　　　—EXODUS 32:24

Jab. Cross. Hook. Uppercut. Repeat. I was in the zone. Enjoying the high of
my cardio kickboxing workout. Pitbull was in the background telling me to
"Give Me Everything," so I did. I went full out with intensity, until I felt the pain
in my jaw from someone who punched me. Dramatic pause—that *someone*
would be me. Instead of uppercutting the air, I punched my own jaw. With no
one to blame, I was forced to come to terms with my own recklessness. I wore
that jaw bruise like a badge of honor, never revealing that it was me who was
the antagonist.

Shifting blame is easy to do when things go wrong. In our sin, it is often
easiest to make excuses for our mistakes or shortcomings. The Bible provides a
spectacular example of this in Exodus 32. The chapter opens by describing the
impatience of God's people when their leader, Moses, went up to Mount Sinai
to have a forty-day meeting with God. "When the cat's away, the mice will play"
is an appropriate description of what was happening when Moses stepped away
from his duties. God's people became very restless with Moses absent and turned
to his brother Aaron, requesting Aaron make "gods" who would take on the
leadership role in the absence of Moses.

God's people completely took advantage of the situation while Moses was away. These false gods they requested from Aaron could never compare to the true God that Moses was away worshiping. Nevertheless, Aaron accepted the challenge, took up a collection of gold jewelry, and constructed a pagan golden calf—a symbol of deity in the ancient world. In other words, they requested a graven image, with complete disregard to the commandment the Lord had given them to not make and worship false gods. God is serious about this command, letting His people know over one hundred times in the Bible to avoid worship of fake gods.

Of all people, Aaron knew better. He knew it was wrong to construct an idol. Instead of standing firm for the Lord—the One True God of Israel—he caved to peer pressure and yielded to a sinful request. When Moses returned to God's people, he witnessed an atrocity. He saw the Lord's followers dancing around the golden calf. In a rage, Moses burned the calf and cast the residue into the drinking water. When Moses asked his brother why he would craft an idol and worship anything other than the Lord, Scripture gives us a model of how ridiculous it sounds when we make excuses for our sin. Aaron answered his brother with the most absurd statement in the Bible. He said, "They gave me this gold, I cast it into the fire, and this calf came out." (Exod. 32:24) By not confessing that he fashioned the calf, he falsely implied that the idol was supernaturally formed. We learn an important lesson about God's character from this text. God wants our truest worship, and he will not condone excuses when we get lazy and try to improvise in our own strength.

Lord, give me a repentant heart when I sin. Forgive me for my desire to have any connection with idols. Allow me the wisdom to confess my poor choices to You and not shift the blame to others. Give me a desire to honor You in my worship. May the gospel of Your grace expose Truth to me in this season. Amen.

-⟫⟫⟫⟩⟨⟨⟨⟨⟨-

God Calls us to Surrender and Trust

For with God nothing will be impossible.

—LUKE 1:37

My Kmart pregnancy test displayed two pink lines after meeting my stream of urine at Lake Johnson Park in Raleigh, North Carolina. It was 2007, and the United States was involved in an ongoing battle to topple the Taliban. My husband, Bryan, had been given an invitation to serve a 12-month assignment in Afghanistan ("they're called 'orders,' Maverick") and I had just dropped him off with his unit moments before the pretty pink lines appeared in the park bathroom to reveal I was pregnant with my daughter, Lucy. An assault of emotions met me: excitement, gratitude, shock, and disbelief.

The Bible also describes a pregnancy reveal. However, unlike the modern image of two pink lines to divulge the exciting news, the Biblical pregnancy unveiling involved a scenario in which an angel visited a young girl named Mary. This disclosure of information was a one-of-a-kind experience unique to Mary because she was favored by God (Luke 1:30).

The angel revealed a few noteworthy details to Mary at this occasion. First, he told her not to be afraid. He let her know that because she found favor with God, she would conceive and bear a son. She was told that his name would be Jesus. It was also revealed to her that God had a great plan for the life of this baby. Mary's only reply was simple and honest. She asked, "how can this be, since I'm a virgin?" (Luke 1:34).

The angel addressed her concerns by giving Mary complete assurance that God's power would lead her through this time. Mary was full of faith and surrendered to God. The Bible gives an astounding model of what our response should be when God presents us with a situation that will demolish any plans we have for our lives. Mary did not expect this news and believed it was not even possible to get pregnant, since she was a virgin. Yet God made a way for the Savior of the World to be born through her. She responds in a way that displays her faith and confidence in the Lord's plan for her life. She acknowledged that she was the Lord's servant and was willing to do whatever God wanted. God's character equips us to understand this precept as we grow in our relationship with Him.

Mary's testimony of her pregnancy reveals a model of servant leadership. Her faith demonstrated that she trusted God, no matter what it cost her. She could have been concerned with her reputation once the news of the pregnancy of an unwed mother hit the streets of Nazareth, but by faith and surrender, she chose to honor God with a joyful heart.

Lord, allow me to have a heart like Mary and respond with willingness when You present a path I did not expect. Help me to surrender my plans into Your will and trust that You will guide my steps. Give me discernment on how to navigate when my steps are redirected and the plans I have made for myself look different than expected. Allow my heart to fully submit to Your will. Amen.

->>>>>?<<<<-

God Will Meet You in Seasons of Darkness

Then Jacob was left alone; and a Man wrestled with him until the breaking of day.

—GENESIS 32:24

Sometimes a one-on-one encounter with God is painful. Ask biblical hero Jacob about this. I have scanned the card racks at Hallmark but, unfortunately, have not had success in finding any verses describing his intense all-night wrestling match with God on a greeting card for encouragement. Nor is it the image you'll typically see on the flannelgraph storytelling board in the church preschool program. However, this was absolutely the most fun verse to model and teach to my son, Luke, when he was a toddler. He showed and received love by reenacting Monday Night Raw with his mama. Never mind that his mama weighed six times more than he did; I wrestled him with the intensity that the Lord wrestled Jacob. This was our favorite bonding activity during the preschool years, and our favorite Bible lesson.

Jacob was 100 years old at the time of the aforementioned grapple described in Genesis 32:22–32. This begs the question—why would God choose to appear in a human form and initiate a physical struggle with this old man? To discover the answer, we need to backtrack to the beginning of Genesis chapter 32.

The scene opens as Jacob is en route back to his homeland. He is accompanied by his four wives and children. After a twenty-year relationship sabbatical from his twin brother, Esau, he finds himself "greatly afraid and distressed" (Gen. 32:7) when he hears through the rumor mill in Canaan that Esau had four hundred men with him. Seeking to avoid complete annihilation, Jacob escapes and spends the night alone in prayer. He prays that God would deliver him from the wrath of his brother who had vowed to kill him.

The history of the conflict between these twins began in the womb and continued through their childhood. They pursued different hobbies (Esau loved hunting, but Jacob preferred tending to animals) and each had a preferred parent they enjoyed spending time with (Esau favored his dad, Jacob favored his mom). However, the primary reason for their twenty year separation was due to differences of opinion on who obtained the birthright blessing (see Gen. 25:31).

Jacob's goal of a solo night in isolation was derailed when God himself appeared in human form and deprived Jacob of his human strength. I love the two details that give context to the meeting—it was night and Jacob was alone. I can relate, having had my most impactful meetings with God alone and in the dark. A solo appointment caused Jacob to face God directly. They wrestled throughout the night until sunrise, when Jacob demanded a blessing from God. In response, God changed his name from Jacob to Israel because he had struggled with God and had prevailed (Gen. 32:28).

Through this biblical brawl, we are faced to come to terms with our own personal elements of struggle. Throughout Genesis, we see glimpses of Jacob's hard life. We become aware of his fears, vulnerabilities, pain, and powerlessness. The encouragement from this story comes when we realize that Jacob faced God and experienced the blessing of real growth through the (literal) struggle and pain.

Lord, meet me in my seasons of struggle. Help me to boldly trust You when I am in despair. Reveal Yourself to me and remind me of Your faithfulness and power to sustain me. When I am weary, I ask that You equip me with Your strength and Your peace to navigate the seasons of challenge. Amen.

-»»»«««-

God's Not Dead

For I consider that the sufferings of this present time are not worthy
to be compared with the glory which shall be revealed in us.
—ROMANS 8:18

God's Not Dead theology became popular at the same time velour jumpsuits came on the scene in the early 2000s. My husband, Bryan, detested this fashion trend and still, twenty years later, experiences heart palpitations when I remind him that he picked me up wearing a velour track suit for our first date. He has suffered several strained eye muscles due to his dramatic eye rolls when I remind him that he fell in love with a thick girl, wearing bubble gum pink velour at an Irish Pub. Like the fashion statement I boldly proclaimed in my trendy attire, "God's Not Dead" theology is unforgettable and highly notable.

The phrase "God's Not Dead" is a book title, a song lyric made popular by the Christian band, *Newsboys*, and later a movie title. The theology is biblical, serving as a complete contrast to Death of God Theology (or Radical Theology) that attracted skeptics of biblical faith in the 1960s. The movement attempted to create a new and improved faith more acceptable to modern men and women. Radical Theology sought to reform the idea of a purely human Christ, rather than a divine incarnate. This is *not* biblical Truth, rather it adheres more closely with postmodernism and ultimately represents an attempt to accommodate secular humanism. By God's grace, the movement lost popularity when the world became aware of the phrase "God's Not Dead," and the 2014 film was released which shares the same title. Several important aspects of Biblical faith are portrayed in this film. Watch the movie. Let the creativity of Hollywood inspire some theological conversations among your peers and challenge your personal beliefs.

The primary theme of this film is originally stated by Paul in his letter to the Romans. He writes on the promises of God and the reality that there is no comparison between the present hard times and the coming good times. The movie highlights the lives of several unrelated characters which all carry the overarching theme of "suffering" in our present circumstances.

The main plot is the story of Josh—a college student—and his outspoken Atheist philosophy professor who requires the entire class to submit a piece of paper with three simple words—God is Dead. When Josh respectfully declines to write these words, he is required to prove to the entire class in a series of lectures that God is *not* Dead. If Josh fails to prove this, he will earn a failing grade.

Through the plot line, we learn the additional details of how Josh "suffers" because of this circumstance and the chain of events caused by his decision to remain steadfast in his walk with Christ. Several other unrelated characters suffer tremendous circumstances for their faith in the film. After viewing this film, we are left with a visual understanding of Paul's message. Paul and the cast of characters in the film remind us that if we choose to focus exclusively on our current sufferings, we will be tempted to lose faith. Paul's words to the Romans remind us that every challenge, hardship, and season of suffering during this present time are not even worth comparing with the glory that will be revealed to us. In other words, this glory we are promised will be revealed to the Christ follower who suffers, just as Jesus suffered.

Lord, give me courage to face the daily challenges that exist on this side of the cross. Allow me the insight to gain glimpses of Your character through my suffering. Teach me that my struggle is nothing compared to the glory of having You as my Savior. Help me be bold for the sake of the Gospel. Amen.

God is a Redeemer

But as for you, you meant evil against me; but God meant it for good,
in order to bring it about as it is this day, to save many people alive.
—GENESIS 50:20

I'm standing by, waiting with great expectation and anticipation for the major motion picture detailing the life of biblical hero, Joseph. I am anxious to discover who will be cast in the role playing my favorite biblical fashion influencer. I expect a young Channing Tatum look alike, due to the fact that the Bible tells us that Joseph had a well-built body and handsome face (Gen. 39:6). If my imagination serves me well and the casting director hits a home run, I see the advertising campaigns, merchandise materials, and billboards attracting a lot of attention for this film.

Joseph was certainly easy on the eyes. But beyond the fact that he was delightfully handsome with an impeccable physique, we also learn that he was the favored of Jacob's twelve sons. To show his favoritism to Joseph, Jacob gave him a unique gift—a multi-colored jacket that Joseph could wear around Canaan adding to his swag. This "tunic of many colors" was the antithesis of brotherly bonding for this family.

Jealousy was the primary sin of the brothers after Papa Jacob gifted Joseph with the new apparel. In anger, the boys sold their brother into slavery. This triggered a multi-layered chain of events that continued to bring hardships to Joseph. As a slave, he worked for one of King Pharaoh's officials, Potiphar.

Potiphar's wife took notice that Joseph had been blessed with an exceptional appearance and tried to seduce him (Gen. 39:12). When he fled from her presence due to his desire to honor God in his purity, her ego was crushed. As a result, she accused Joseph of rape. This resulted in an immediate prison sentence through no fault of his own.

The next ten chapters of Genesis describe how God accomplished many wonderful things throughout the seemingly difficult set of circumstances that Joseph endured. Over a period of 13 years, God ordained a series of highs and lows for Joseph to be used in the Lord's plan. Genesis 50:20 serves as an encouraging reminder about God's character. In this verse, Joseph tells his brothers that even though they intended to harm him, God used that circumstance for good.

Remarkably, Joseph was able to forget the pain and suffering he experienced through the poor choices of his brothers and see that the Lord used the hardships for His glory. When we examine the highs and lows of our lives, perhaps we can say the same. God eventually elevated Joseph to a top leadership position in Egypt and reunited him with his family. The story of Joseph's life is a remarkable testimony of how God is completely sovereign over all the details and experiences of our lives, even when circumstances do not seem ideal.

Lord, allow me to remember this verse on how Your sovereign plan will be used to accomplish Your gracious purposes in my life. Like Joseph, allow me to forgive those who have hurt me and be bold for Your glory in challenging times. Give me Your wisdom on how to navigate challenging relationships with family members. Amen.

———————— ->>>>><<<<<- ————————

God Pursues You

I say to you that likewise there will be more joy in heaven over one sinner who repents than over ninety-nine just persons who need no repentance.

—_LUKE 15:7_

The love of God is available to everyone. People of all _sheeps_ and sizes, colors, income levels, political parties, and nationalities. Geographically, God does not limit his jurisdiction. He does not bypass seeking those who have known a life of rebellion. God deeply loves and cares personally for _all_ people.

He graciously provided a visual object lesson of this character trait for me when He brought me to the Prayer March of 2020 in Washington DC. How ironic that one of the best things I have done in my faith _walk_ was attend the _Prayer March_? It was on that day that God provided a visual for me to reveal His character trait of inclusiveness. I was astounded among the swarms of people at the Lincoln Memorial. Until that day, it had been easy for me to think that every Christ follower looked alike. However, here is what I saw: a young guy with a greasy man-bun, an older women wearing a haube and cape dress, a middle-aged guy with face tats and gauges, a young couple with an infant looking like the baby was still covered in vernix—and this was just the group of believers who were within arms reach of me. I was humbled that the kingdom of believers was so visually diverse, and that Jesus _loves ALL of us so well._

Luke 15 opens with a parable where wildlife is used to ram home the point to the erroneous flock of people who were misunderstood regarding who the love of God extends to. The text describes an interesting picture of the people Jesus attracted, stating that "sinners drew near to Him." How astounding that God's own son had credibility and a reputation for hanging out with people who operated outside the margins of society. This threw the religious leaders—known as Pharisees—into a tizzy. The Pharisees were considered to be model church leaders at the time Christ lived on earth. They filed their complaints with the Good Shepherd himself, baffled that He would even entertain the company of those who seemed far from God.

The message to the religious leaders was explicitly clear when Jesus made the point to these people with a parable that explained the joy in heaven when one person says yes to Christ. The parable describes a lost sheep. The shepherd leaves his ninety-nine other sheep to seek the one sheep who was lost. This is not at the expense of the ninety-nine, but indicates God's commitment to each individual person, especially when it comes to danger.

At the time Jesus lived, a vocation in shepherding was a popular career choice. People knew that sheep were very dependent animals and if one went astray from the flock, it was not likely to survive. Since Jesus himself uses the title of "Good Shepherd" to describe himself (John 10:11), the narrative is completely accurate. Like the actual shepherd, Jesus will graciously care for those who wander, and most importantly, rejoice when one of His sheep returns to Him.

Throughout the Bible we notice a recurring theme—people are compared to sheep. It is not a flattering juxtaposition when you break down the key traits of a sheep. They are not intelligent, wander easily, and are known for their stubbornness. Eeek, I realize I've described myself at various seasons during my experience as a Christ follower. Fortunately, God is a gracious and merciful God who lovingly guides us back to Him, just like a shepherd does for his sheep.

Lord, remind me of this parable when I struggle to remember how valuable I am to You. Forgive me for all of the times I have strayed away and acted like a sheep. Thank you for remaining faithful and for coming after me when I lose my way. Amen.

God Can Reshape You

"Arise and go down to the potter's house, and there I will cause you to hear My words."

—*JEREMIAH 18:2*

C lay is a dirty four-letter word. Ironically, it is exactly what the Bible uses to describe God's people. The one and only time I attempted clay crafting on a potter's wheel, the clay had its own idea of how my janky vessel would look. My pottery gift was almost as comical as the passionate scene that takes place over the pottery wheel in the 1990 movie *Ghost*. Just like the pottery crafting was abandoned in the heat of passion when a shirtless Patrick Swayze approached the wheel, my pottery was abandoned when I realized my talents were better suited discussing the biblical metaphor instead of actually participating in the earthenware development process.

God uses a mucky crafting material as a symbol in a message to His people in Jeremiah 18. He instructed the prophet Jeremiah to rise and visit a potter's house for a visual lesson on the relationship between God and His people. This relationship is the primary focus of Jeremiah's writing—the challenged relationship between God and His people. The same message the prophet wrote millennia ago is relevant, necessary, and critical today. From reading the words written by Jeremiah, we gain insight into what our life looks like without God.

We are shapeless and formless until the potter gets involved. In the same way the potter molds the clay, God works on us. The potter prepares the clay to be made into something new. This imagery is a visual reminder of the sanctification process that occurs in our lives when we submit to His molding. The clay yields to the potter's hands after pressure, time, and a plan is put into action. This is a creative metaphor on how we can be changed into the ideal image that God has for our life if we allow Him to shape us. The Bible says we are the work of His hand (Jer. 18:6).

God created us in His image, just the way He wanted us. Our responsibility is to use that creation for His glory. Just as the clay finds purpose when it is pliable in the hands of the potter, our life will accomplish its purpose when we let the potter have His way with us. The Dutch author and speaker Corrie Ten Boom said, "You see, a potter can only mold the clay when it lies completely in His hand. It requires complete surrender."[1] Let this reminder of surrender boldly direct our mindset when we acknowledge that one of God's most impressive character traits is that He *can* reshape us into a far better version of ourselves than we could have ever imagined.

Lord, allow my heart to be open and willing to be molded by You, the perfect potter. Give me strength to be open to Your artistic vision. Allow me to see a season of being fired in the kiln as transformation, not punishment. Bless me with the ability to surrender my life to Your design. Amen.

---

1   Corrie Ten Boom. AZQuotes.com, Wind and Fly LTD, 2023. https://www.azquotes.com/quote/927630, accessed August 18, 2023.

-›››᠈›‹‹‹‹‹-

God is the Author of Real Love

Love suffers long and is kind; love does not envy; love does not parade
itself, is not puffed up; does not behave rudely, does not seek its own, is
not provoked, thinks no evil; does not rejoice in iniquity, but rejoices
in the truth; bears all things, believes all things, hopes all things,
endures all things.

—1 CORINTHIANS 13:4–7

I started middle school in the fall of 1992 in a cool windbreaker track suit. It was the same year the Chicago Bulls won the NBA championship, 2G mobile phones were launched, Kris Kross became famous for wearing clothes backwards, and the world became privy to hearing Mary J. Blige sing about how she was searching for *Real Love*. The song was a huge hit (like my jewel-colored track suit) and peaked at number seven on the US Billboard Hot 100. However, Mary J. Blige was not the first to boldly proclaim the woes of searching for "real love." Thousands of years prior to her song being certified Gold by the Recording Industry Association of America (RIAA), the discussion of real love became a hot topic among the Evangelism Industry Association of Corinth (EIAC).

Like the R&B singer, the apostle Paul used his platform to share some encouraging words on the topic of real love. Although the topic they spoke about was the same, it is important to note that popular culture views love very differently than how the Bible views love. In our society, love is something that happens to us (like falling in love) and usually is associated with feelings and emotions. That was certainly true during the season when Bryan Weber courted me and gushed his feelings through written words that now fill a 2-inch binder documenting our season of falling in love. However, when the Bible speaks of love, it functions as a verb rather than a noun. This means that biblical love is demonstrated and acted out. God's character is the model for how love is demonstrated.

The love passage in 1 Corinthians 13 is well recognized and often read at weddings. It is also one of the most misunderstood passages in the Bible. These verses have been associated with the love between a man and a woman; however, the use of the Greek word agape in this context sheds light on the intended meaning of these verses. Agape means putting the needs of other people ahead of self. Paul's purpose in using the word love is to encourage his readers to attend to the needs of others. By the power of the Holy Spirit, love is the heart of our experience in Christ. While marriage is a great context for practicing this, Paul's desire in writing was to encourage the Corinthian believers to model God's love to others. He meant modeling it to other people in the family of faith, as well as people in the region of Corinth who were outside the faith.

The characteristics Paul used to describe love (patient, kind, not jealous, not irritable, not envious) are only possible by God's grace, when we put others before ourselves and make love a verb. Paul wanted the people of Corinth to know this was a way of life for those who follow Jesus. He wanted them to know that they were using their spiritual gifts apart from love. Paul makes an important point that even these God given gifts amount to nothing if love is not the first priority.

At the time Paul wrote these words, Corinth was a prosperous city of trade and commerce, but spiritually dead due to the influence of pagan traditions. Sexual immorality was rampant, and Paul had a heart to reveal the truth of God's love and character to the early Christians. His words on love are still just as important today as we navigate the Truth of God's Word in the twenty-first century.

Lord, by Your grace, allow me to model the character traits that Your Word describes as real love. Help me to seek after You and rejoice in the fact that Your love bears all things, hopes all things, endures all things, and that Your love never fails. Give me a mind and a heart to make love a verb. Help me to love others well who do not know the character of Christ. Amen.

-》》》》《《《《-

God Loves Your Prayers

Then the king said to me, "What do you request?" So I prayed to the
God of heaven.

—NEHEMIAH 2:4

E ven with a misspelled word on my campaign fliers (Vote Annie for *Presidnet!*) the students of Grosse Pointe North High still somehow found the grace to overlook my negligence and voted me into the prestigious position of Student Council President my senior year. This allowed me and the other leaders the great privilege of delivering the daily announcements over the loudspeaker in our principal's office. I still remember her gentle correction when we got a little foolish one morning and the entire student body heard our nonsensical banter ("please remember, your job is to inform, not to entertain the student body"). This leadership experience was my first exposure to the high calling of serving others, and I had a lot to learn. By God's grace, my leadership capabilities have been drastically reformed since my teenage years. Perhaps it is a combination of maturity, along with life experiences, and my transition into becoming a born-again believer (see Astounding Truth #14) that has strengthened my skill set.

God provides an exceptional model for people in positions of influence through His character in the book of Nehemiah. The book is named after its central figure and provides an early case study in strategic management. Nehemiah was a government worker, employed by a foreign king. He later transitioned into a career as a building contractor who was tasked with rebuilding the walls of Jerusalem after they were destroyed (see 2 Chron. 36:19).

Nehemiah was gifted with an array of leadership strategies which ranged from perseverance to prayer. By knowing the story of Nehemiah's life, we gain an understanding of what a godly leader looks like and how God works sovereignly through His people to accomplish His redemptive plans.

Nehemiah 2 opens with Nehemiah completing one of his duties as a public servant—taste testing the wine of the king. This duty serves as an indication that Nehemiah was a trustworthy leader, as his job was to ensure the drinks were free from poison. This task triggered an important conversation for Nehemiah that first involved prayer. Verse 4 serves as an important reminder that leaders are to first go to God in prayer before making decisions. With God's blessing, Nehemiah then asked his boss, King Artaxerxes, for time off work, a travel visa, and building supplies to rebuild the walls of Jerusalem. Miraculously, the king granted all the requests and went above and beyond by sending military officers to assist with the task. Nehemiah did what successful leaders do—he leveraged his power for God's glory and to his advantage. The king granted his requests because he had a reputation for integrity. God honors our commitment to having strong moral principles, as we see modeled by Nehemiah.

Upon arriving in Jerusalem, Nehemiah formed a plan. He got immediately to work, allowed no distractions, and told no one what God had put on his heart to do (see Neh. 2:12). Sometimes we can embark on the tasks God has called us to without telling anyone first. My suspicion is that Nehemiah was so affected by the gravity of the rebuilding project, that he needed to quietly assess to gain a full understanding of God's calling for him. Oh, how I can relate.

The Bible tells us that Nehemiah took only his donkey, and when the landscape allowed for unsafe conditions for the animal to pass, Nehemiah had to get off his donkey and walk. How good is God to provide a reminder that like Nehemiah, we'll need to get off our ass to accomplish the Kingdom work that God has assigned us.

Lord, allow me to be faithful in the calling You have placed on my life. Like Nehemiah, allow me to persevere for Your glory and do what it takes to accomplish Your will by faithfully praying for Your favor. I humbly ask for no distractions. Help me hear from you regarding the direction you would like me to go, what to do, and how to pray. Amen.

-》》》》《《《《-

God Offers Rebirth

Jesus answered and said to him, "Most assuredly, I say to you, unless one is born again, he cannot see the kingdom of God."

—*JOHN 3:3*

John 3 opens with an introduction about a man named Nicodemus. He is my biblical desired doppelganger (German word which literally means *double walker²*). Nicodemus and I share similar personality traits. We both are truth seekers. We inquire and we question the same beliefs. We are highly curious (my husband enjoys reminding me that every interaction with a new person does NOT need to be an interview). Finally, we are both cautious when faced with the truth of believing who Christ is.

Nicodemus is known for springboarding the most quoted verse in the Bible—John 3:16. The conversation between Jesus and Nicodemus that led to this famous verse (with the help of Tim Tebow) was birthed because Nicodemus was highly unsatisfied with the legalism of the Pharisees. These people were loyal to the Old Testament law, but unfortunately, opposed the teaching of Jesus. They struggled to understand the depth of why Jesus came and what He came to do. In today's terms, this would be like a person seeking righteousness by checking certain boxes, but completely ignoring crucial heart matters. I completely relate

---

2   *Vocabulary.com Dictionary*, s.v. "doppelganger," accessed August 17, 2023, https://www.vocabulary.com/dictionary/doppelganger.

to the emotion of the Pharisees. Being a prominent Pharisee himself, he avoided seeking Jesus in the daylight for fear of how his peers would react, instead meeting with him at night. Nicodemus was hungry for Truth straight from the source.

In John 3:3, we read the red-letter words of Jesus who says, "unless one is born again, he cannot see the kingdom of God." His reply ("how can a man be born when he is old? Can he enter a second time into his mother's womb and be born?") has always struck me as entirely honest and relatable. Maybe it was exhaustion from the lateness of the hour, but he struggled to understand. Like Nicodemus, I also struggled with the phrase "born again" when I first heard it as a teenager, before I understood that this strange combination of words came from the mouth of Jesus. Nicodemus said exactly what I thought when I first heard someone ask if I was "born again." How is it possible to be born *again?*

Jesus graciously taught Nicodemus an important lesson that every person needs to hear. When we are born (via our mother's womb) we are actually born *dead.* Even with breath in our lungs, a beating heart, and a ten on the Apgar Test, we are born spiritually dead. Jesus explained that rebirth is an essential part of the faith journey toward Christ. During this second birth, a person encounters the Holy Spirit. This is more than having salvation in Christ. It means you are a completely new person in Christ. The words Jesus spoke to Nicodemus are a stark reminder that only by experiencing a second birth are we assured of seeing the kingdom of God.

Lord, Thank You for the refinement I can experience in the process of spiritual rebirth. Through this process, I am able to see the old me being replaced by a new me with You, Lord, guiding my path. I ask You to come into my heart and make me a new person in Christ. Amen.

-))))((((-

God Hears Our Groaning

*So God heard their groaning, and God remembered His covenant
with Abraham, with Isaac, and with Jacob. And God looked upon
the children of Israel, and God acknowledged them.*
—EXODUS 2:24–25

The temperature was ninety-two degrees with three hundred percent
humidity. I had a sudden enthusiastic desire to search for the infamous
Genie Rocks of Guam. The search was a success but required a trek through a
jungle path covered with dried coral remnants. Levi, my three-year-old adventure
companion groaned, his response considerably less enthusiastic than mine. Little
Levi's acknowledgment of this ambitious pursuit is not foreign. It is our fleshly
desire to groan when we experience circumstances that are uncomfortable,
difficult, or downright unpleasant. The Bible describes a situation when God's
people groaned in a challenging season. By examining the text, we gain a kingdom
perspective on trekking through difficult circumstances, just like little Levi was
forced to endure with his adventurous mama.

Exodus 2 describes the charmed early life of Moses. He lived as a royal in
Pharaoh's home, educated among the elite of Egypt. This chapter also explains
how God prepared Moses to serve as the appointed leader of the Hebrew people.
God gave Moses the gift of mercy. Even though Moses grew up with privilege, he
had a strong desire to care for God's people—his true heritage. At age forty, Moses
became privy to the truths about how poorly his people were treated. When he

witnessed an Egyptian beating someone in the family of God, he reacted with an extreme response. Moses murdered the thug, disposed of the body in the sand, and escaped to a foreign land about 300 miles away (Exod. 2:12).

The chapter ends with a description which vaguely reminds us of the aforementioned toddler groaning about the trail. Exodus 2:23 describes God's people groaning because their slave labor was so difficult. They were desperate to leave their time in slavery and return to the land promised by God. This text serves as an invitation to do the same when we find ourselves in a season of bondage or difficult circumstances.

The Bible says, "God heard their groaning and remembered His covenant… And God acknowledged them." We see an example here of God's character: His divine faithfulness to the covenant promises he made to his people. While the deliverance did not occur on the timeline of the Hebrew people, during that season of waiting in the wilderness forty years, they focused on the faithfulness of the Lord and kept their attention on Him. That testimony should always be our model when we trudge through a season of trial.

Lord, allow me to have a kingdom perspective when waking through a difficult season or wilderness. Help me to remember that You always hear my groans and provide a solution according to Your perfect plan. You are Jehovah Shalom: the God of peace. Remind me that nothing else can bring me the comfort and peace that You can provide during a storm. Amen.

->>>>)<<<<-

God's Plan is Not Classified Information

The mystery which has been hidden from ages and from generations, but now has been revealed to His saints.

—COLOSSIANS 1:26

To celebrate the momentous occasion of my husband's fortieth trip around the sun, I planned a surprise celebration in his honor. Several of his colleagues, who were also federal employees, were included in the festivities. To keep consistent with the surprise celebration theme, I emailed the party details with the subject line stating "CLASSIFIED" in boldface letters. Weeks later, after we had recovered from the carb fest brought on by Chipotle burritos, I was made aware that my email caused a moment of panic when it was discovered that a "CLASSIFIED" email was received in unsecure inboxes. Lesson learned: My wry personality remains distant from anyone with a top-secret clearance.

Long before email was available, the apostle Paul wrote an encouraging letter from prison to a group of people he had never met. This letter is now called the book of Colossians. It was a love letter filled with encouragement, truthful theology, and warning against forgetting that Christ is *all* you need for salvation. Paul wrote this letter to also communicate a critical detail—the message of Christ is *not* classified information. At the time this letter was written, pagan religions were highly influential to groups of new Christians. Pagan religions had "classified" insights that were only available to a few select people, usually for a fee. One of Paul's main purposes for writing Colossians was to clarify that

Christ lives in *every* believer. No fee is needed to receive the gift of Christ. Every person is welcome into the family of God, regardless of clearance.

As an added bonus, this letter also included a message regarding mental wellness. He tells the people of Colossae to set their minds to things above (Col. 3:2). Paul's message is incredibly relevant today, two thousand years after his letter was sent. He intends for us to be keenly aware of looking at things from God's perspective. Followers of Christ must be tuned into the Kingdom Broadcasting Network (KBN) to receive wisdom on how to live a life that honors God. Paul essentially says to turn off the message of the pagan world and hear the Truth of Christ.

When tuned into programming that is not Christ-centered, it becomes easy to be swayed by messages that are contradictory to what the Bible teaches about kingdom living. Paul is reminding the believers at Colossae and the believers of the twenty-first century to take a heavenly perspective on every circumstance you face. He encouraged his ancient audience to become aware of their sinful lives that came naturally before knowing Jesus. He charged them to participate in a rigorous and radical departure from their old sinful lives and rejoice in the new life that Christ has allowed for them.

Lord, I praise You for revealing the Truth of your character to all people. Your Word tells us that the message of Jesus is available for everyone, regardless of their religious standing. Allow me to receive Your message with open arms, to keep my mind and eyes toward thoughts of You, and be alert toward what You are revealing to me. Amen.

-》》》》《《《《-

God Uses Broken People for Kingdom Purposes

The Lord is close to the brokenhearted; he rescues those whose spirits are crushed.

—PSALM 34:18, NLT

Genesis 38 tells the story about Tamar, a gal whose name means "Palm Tree." Palm trees are my preferred perennials, my favorite foliage to admire, displayed on my best-loved Pottery Barn duvet cover, and the inspiration for my book cover design. However, unlike my favorite tree, the palm described in the Bible does not trigger the same breezy feelings brought on by palm branches waving along the oceanside.

Scripture tells us that Tamar posed as a prostitute and solicited sexual relations with her faither-in-law, Judah (Gen. 38:16). I have yet to see the preschool coloring page for this chapter of Scripture when I volunteer to serve in children's ministry at church. I don't suppose people are lining up to play Tamar in the church play. This chapter is dark, yet the astounding revelation we gain from this story is how God chose to redeem Tamar and use her in the genealogy of Jesus. In our flesh, it is often unimaginable to think that God would use such broken and sinful humans in the line of Christ. Nevertheless, the Lord used people like Tamar and other rebels to teach us about His character.

Tamar had a tragic backstory. Judah and his wife had three sons. Er was the oldest, and his name makes me wonder if Er is short for *error*. The Bible tells us that Er was wicked in the sight of the Lord, and the Lord killed him (Gen. 38:7). After his death, Er's wife, Tamar, was passed on to Er's next younger brother, Onan, to produce an offspring for Er. This was a customary practice during this time, to have a widow marry the next brother. Widows were not allowed to marry outside the family. The goal was for Tamar to have a son who would carry on Er's name and inherit his land. Onan was now responsible for producing a son for Tamar. Judging from the context clues we gather from Genesis 38:9 (read the verse!), he was not thrilled about being used to provide an offspring for his big brother, Er.

We learn a few verses later about the character of God—He does not condone wickedness. When brother #2 prevented Tamar from conceiving, he got the same consequences as brother #1. God knew that this was unfair to Er and Tamar, and put Onan to death for his cunning practices. Judah decided to take matters into his own hands and withheld son #3 from Tamar. Since she was still "married" to the family, she had no other options for love or offspring. She was sent back home to live with her parents (Gen. 38:11) full of shame and disgrace.

If the story was a stage play, this is where we would be invited to stand and get snacks during intermission. A long time passes as the second act opens, and we learn that Judah has now also become a widower. Tamar was notified that her father-in-law Judah was traveling her way to shear his sheep. Tamar was more concerned with being a mother than living righteously. Her life was hard living as a quasi-widow because she was most likely shunned by society. Since no sperm bank appeared to be in operation, she took matters into her own hands, disguising herself and pretending to be a prostitute as Judah approached. She became pregnant by him (Gen. 38:24), and Judah found out three months later. Tamar was slick in her plans and found a way to trap Judah and prove to everyone that he was the rightful father. Judah was at a crossroads, faced with the revelation that he was now the father of this baby. At this point, we see the story end with a dramatic conclusion. Judah acknowledged his shortcoming, and we learn that Tamar was commended for her daring efforts to build up her family.

Lord, help me to remember that Your will is sometimes accomplished by messy human relationships. Redemption is possible for everyone, and today I thank you for redeeming me from my sinful ways. Thank you for your grace. Help me be wise in navigating situations where I am challenged to see how my brokenness can be used for Kingdom purposes, as modeled in the life of Tamar. Amen.

-϶϶϶϶϶Ͻ϶ϹϹϹϹϹ-

God Saves

*If you confess with your mouth the Lord Jesus and believe in your heart
that God has raised Him from the dead, you will be saved.*

—ROMANS 10:9

My childhood pastime included watching *Saved by the Bell* reruns. A penny *saved* is a penny earned. My laptop can operate in power *saving* mode. We receive postcards in the mail asking us to "*Save* the Date" for an upcoming wedding celebration. We are reminded to *save* water by taking shorter showers. A life preserver can *save* a life when someone cannot swim.

With so many nuanced meanings of the word "*saved*" in our culture, why do some shudder at the question "are you saved?" The first time I heard that question, I was baffled. It was not a phrase I was familiar with, even though I regularly attended church since I departed from the womb.

The word "saved" in the Biblical context is a word that some faith traditions do not use when describing the process of acknowledging that Jesus died as a complete price paid for our sin. *How* we are saved is crucial, but more importantly *who* does the saving is the essential piece of the puzzle.

To understand why we need a Savior, we must understand God's plan for humanity. God set a nonnegotiable boundary for Adam and Eve regarding the fruit on the tree of the knowledge of good and evil (see Gen. 2:17). Their craving for some simple carbohydrates exiled them from the perfect environment of the garden and brought spiritual death. That one act of disobedience—eating the forbidden fruit—redirected God's plan for His people. As a result, all humans received the disappointing trait of complete sin nature. This means that regardless of how hard we try to be good, we are unable. Our natural tendency to prioritize serving self (rather than God) and our constant desire to sin is due to the circumstances we were all born into.

God in His infinite wisdom provided a perfect solution for this detour—sending His son Jesus to die for our sins. It is through Him alone that we are saved. In Romans 10:9, Paul writes, "that if you confess with your mouth the Lord Jesus and believe in your heart that God has raised Him from the dead, you will be saved." We are "saved" not by how good we are, but because we acknowledge that Jesus died for us as a complete price paid for our sin. This means no layaway, no payment plan, no pay as you go—PAID IN FULL. This allows us an opportunity to be in Heaven with him for eternity. We should have been hung on the cross, but Jesus took our place.

Lord, I acknowledge that I cannot save myself. Your promise of salvation was true yesterday, today, and every day in the future. I trust You to forgive my sin and give me eternal life. Thank you for this free gift of salvation which allows me a place in heaven with You forever. I ask that You equip me with the tools I need to be bold with this message to the people You have trusted me to care for. Amen.

God is Praiseworthy

"Naked I came from my mother's womb, And naked shall I return there. The Lord gave and the Lord has taken away; Blessed be the name of the Lord."

—*JOB 1:21*

Let's cringe together as I recall the awkward embarrassment I felt when a friend texted me with the news that her pastor was teaching from the book of Job. The uncomfortable part came when we spoke later and I asked her about Job, as is paid employment. To be clear, I have since learned that the book of the Bible and the text describing the principal character is about a man named Job (long o, rhymes with robe). In his book, which kicks off the section of scripture known as the Poetic Books of the Bible, we learn about the *exposed* truth of his faith.

The book of Job raises some of the greatest questions about theological issues on why righteous people suffer and opens with a fun fact that is *Guinness Book of World Records* worthy—*Job was the godliest man on earth*. Terms like *blameless* and *upright* are used to describe Job (Job 1:8). However, God in his providence allowed Satan to test this faithful man. Through the book of Job, we get a comprehensive tutorial on how to combat the issues of loss and suffering by reading how Job responded with frankness toward God. The astounding truth about Job's life is how he continued to praise God through the extreme trial of losing everything.

Every human will experience suffering—hardships with family, health challenges, material loss, broken relationships, financial crisis, breach in trust, shattered dreams—these circumstances cannot be avoided because we live in a world with sin. Job lost his entire family, his animals, his servants, and his property, yet he chose to not lose his faith and instead to see how God's hand was involved in every circumstance of his life. He acknowledged that God was doing something in his life that was better for him.

Perhaps God intended to build Job's faith by allowing him to wait and keep praying. We benefit tremendously from the bare truth that Job lamented in verse 1:21, "Naked I came from my mother's womb, And Naked shall I return there. The Lord gave and the Lord has taken away; Blessed be the name of the Lord." This is a poetic way of saying that everything we have belongs to the Creator who gave it. Upon realizing that everything was taken from him, Job confessed that everything he had was from God, so God had the right to take it away. This is a stark contrast to the world's view on obtaining wealth, material possessions, and successes. Everything you have been blessed with, your skills, resources, and people in your life are God's gifts to you.

Lord, allow me to be at peace when Your will does not align with my will. Help me remember that You are praiseworthy, even during the storms of life. Help me to receive with grace the gifts You have given me and remain faithful like Job when hard times come. Blessed be the name of the Lord! Amen.

-›››››‹‹‹‹-

God is Consistent

But avoid foolish disputes, genealogies, contentions, and strivings about the law; for they are unprofitable and useless.

—TITUS 3:9

When I attended Monteith Elementary School in the nineties, our solar system had nine planets. That fact is not taught today at McCool School on US Naval Base Guam, where my kids currently attend. None of the remaining eight planets in our solar system have shown an interest in keeping up a relationship with Pluto since he was kicked out in 2006. Apparently, Pluto was just too cold and distant. The International Astronomical Union made the decision to downgrade the status of Pluto to a dwarf planet based on research that proved inconsistent from previous years.[3] Science is—at times—inconsistent. However, God is *never* inconsistent.

The New Testament opens with the genealogy of Jesus. If you shook that family tree of Jesus, plenty of nuts would fall out. As Matthew lists the ancestors of Jesus, he makes an excellent case for grace. God used many unlikely people in the lineage of Jesus. This list includes a prostitute (Rahab), a pretend prostitute (Tamar), and other broken individuals who were not of Jewish descent (Bathsheba and Ruth). Because Matthew intentionally listed many unlikely ancestors cf Jesus,

---

3   Hogeback, J.. "Why Is Pluto No Longer a Planet?." *Encyclopedia Britannica*, September 16, 2016. https://www.britannica.com/story/why-is-pluto-no-longer-a-planet.

it is a prime example that the Lord's plan does not depend on human worthiness. God sovereignly chooses who He uses to orchestrate His plan of redemption. So, is it a contradiction when the apostle Paul speaks *against* genealogies in two of his letters?

God's word will never contradict itself. It is important that we look at the context in which Paul is communicating with his friends Timothy and Titus. In Paul's first letter to Timothy , he writes a warning against listening to false teachers who promote lies (1 Tim. 1:4). He warns his audience to not let false teachers waste their time with endless discussions of myths and spiritual pedigrees. Since Jesus had already come, the separation between God's people and pagan people was no longer necessary. We are all alike when we are in the family of Christ. Paul emphasized that the early followers of Christ needed to stop favoring the Jewish people who were known as God's people for thousands of years. He also asked them to stop marginalizing the Gentiles (those who were not of Jewish descent) because the blood of Jesus was shed for *all*.

The message was repeated in Paul's letter to Titus with even greater urgency. Paul says genealogies are foolish because of their impractical nature (Titus 3:9). He also warned of the damage done by flaunting your lineage. We are not to have pride in our ancestry, but rather we should boast about having Christ (see insights on boasting in 1 Cor. 15:31 and 2 Cor. 7:4). Paul knew that historically, the Jewish people may have been prone to arrogance because of who their ancestors were. Paul desired clarity regarding biblical genealogies. They have a vital purpose in demonstrating the Lord's faithfulness through generations, but are no longer necessary to invest time into, because they are unprofitable and useless in the advancement of the Gospel.

Lord, I praise You today for the New Covenant allowing all people to rejoice in the unity that Jews and Gentiles now share. Thank You for Your Word and for calling me into Your family through faith in Christ. Allow me Your confidence to boast in who I am because of the work You have done in my life, making me more like Christ. Amen.

~->>>>?<<<<~

God is Faithful Toward the Rebellious

Come, and let us return to the Lord; for He has torn, but He will heal us; He has stricken, but He will bind us up.

—*HOSEA 6:1*

Thanks to the creative literary talent of best-selling author Francine Rivers, I was exposed to a fictional retelling of the redemptive story of Hosea in her book *Redeeming Love*. Her writing is utterly heart wrenching, and she did a marvelous job glorifying God through this fictional story. Her book found its way into my hands in a time when I did not understand God's redemptive character, but I got a glimpse of it through her innovative talent. This accomplished author began her writing career in the historical romance genre before she met Jesus. When she became a Christian, her time studying the Bible led her to transition into writing Christian themes. Her first novel in this vein, *Redeeming Love,* was wildly successful (selling over three million copies and translated into thirty languages). The fame of this story continued in 2022 when it hit the silver screen.

The book of Hosea completely transcends human understanding. Hosea uniquely illustrates how beautifully and painfully God loves us. It kicks off with a direct command from God to Hosea, "Go, take yourself a wife of harlotry, and have children of harlotry, for the land has committed great harlotry" (Hosea 1:2). Say what—Did we read this correctly? Why would God command the prophet Hosea to marry a prostitute?

The message of the book of Hosea is multiplied through the use of imagery. The metaphors used derive from the human experience of intimacy. Through the image of marriage and family life, Hosea depicts God and His relationship with His people. The underlying theme is consistent throughout the book: God's people, the nation of Israel, broke the covenant that God made when He redeemed them from Egypt. Hosea lovingly refers to Israel as "your mother" several times throughout the book (see Astounding Truth #51 for another Biblical Yo Mama reference).

The more God's people departed from God, the more He called after them (Hosea 11:2). The broken covenant relationship was represented by the unhappy marriage relationship between Hosea and his wife. Although she was unfaithful many times, Hosea lovingly took her back as his beloved wife and extended her grace. Her unfaithfulness symbolizes how God's people were unfaithful to the Lord. It parallels God's consistent activity of restoring His people after numerous unfaithful adventures.

This story about fidelity and faithfulness shows us that God's character never wavered in his covenant loyalty to His people. Hosea 14, the final chapter shows us the miracle of God's love displayed by Him when He offered a fresh start with his people. His love is relentless toward us. No matter how many times we stray, He will always welcome us back with open arms.

Lord, bring restoration from my unfaithfulness and rebellion. The testimony from the book of Hosea reminds me that I also have been unfaithful at times. I repent from my infidelity and ask that You redeem my past. I pray that I walk in the spirit of Your truth and grow in obedience. Allow me to see the depth of Your love for me. Amen.

-》》》》《《《-

God Provides Redirection

And anyone not found written in the Book of Life was cast into the
lake of fire.

—REVELATION 20:15

B orn and raised in Michigan, I love Great Lakes swimming. Unsalted and
shark free is my favorite aquatic environment to spend the lazy days of
summer. My best childhood memories were on Lake Huron, my most memorable
college moments were alongside Lake Michigan, and my most tender adult
moments were near Lake Superior surrounded by my Yooper family.

The apostle John also had some thoughts to share about lake life. However,
the lake he wrote of is not one where we would desire to plan our next vacation,
filling our digital scrapbooks with cherished photos. He writes of the lake of
fire, which is another phrase to describe hell, the final destination of those who
reject Christ.

Why would a good God send someone to hell? I'm so glad you asked this
important question. It is a question I have heard people ask with sincerity and
curiosity, seeking an honest answer in order to understand the Christian faith.
The astounding truth about the Lord and His choice to send someone to hell may
be shocking to you: *God does not send people to hell.* The truth is, we are already
on our way to hell. What God does for us is provide an alternative solution. He
provided a way to escape our fiery destination by providing His Son, Jesus.

The 1997 film *Titanic* does an excellent job of giving the viewer a visual object lesson of what this looks like. As the sinking vessel fell further and deeper in the northern Atlantic Ocean, lifeboats were launched. Captain Smith refused to get aboard the lifeboat, thus he went down with the ship. Like the sinking vessel, our sin was already taking us to hell. God gave us Jesus as a lifeboat to save us from eternal separation from God.

The Lord gave humanity the best gift of all when God sent His Son to take all the punishment for our brokenness, shortcomings, and failures—what the Bible calls sin. No matter how hard we try to live a perfect life, we are not capable of living as God intended for us to live, because we are separated from God during our season on earth. By making the choice to get on the lifeboat, we choose heaven as our final and forever destination because of the work done on the cross over two thousand years ago in Calvary.

By making a choice to not get on the lifeboat provided by God—which is completely free—you are choosing eternal separation from God. Jude verse 7 (the book of Jude only has one chapter) describes hell as suffering the vengeance of eternal fire. Other biblical descriptions include gnashing of teeth, burning sulfur, and complete darkness. One of the Bible's greatest truths is that God offers this free gift to all people. Go ahead, get on the lifeboat and thank God for His amazing provision of His Son, Jesus.

Lord, I thank You today for the blessing of providing redirection through your Son, Jesus. I recognize my need for this gift and choose to accept it with joy and appreciation. I accept You as Lord and Savior. Thank you for providing a perfect solution for the brokenness of our world. Amen.

God Will Never Leave You

Though I walk through the valley of the shadow of death, I will fear no evil; For You are with me; Your rod and Your staff, they comfort me.
—*PSALM 23:4*

I was unfamiliar with the Bible when I heard Coolio sing a borrowed lyric from Psalm 23:4 to open his chart-topping song "Gangsta's Paradise." The song won a Grammy Award and was the best-selling single of 1995. It was released in conjunction with the film *Dangerous Minds*, which highlights the challenges of teaching underachieving teens in an inner-city high school. Coolio included the psalm lyric to evoke feelings about the challenges of life as a gangster in southern California.

On the contrary, King David wrote Psalm 23 as a declaration of trust and confidence in God's character. David is boldly professing his complete confidence that God's character will be consistent every day of his life. By writing this Psalm, he acknowledged God's track record of caring for His people. This includes every individual sheep that has been placed in His care.

David had the advantage of looking back over his life and seeing how God cared for him through the seasons of character refinement he experienced. In writing this Psalm, he expressed his genuine thoughts on how he evaluated his relationship with God. This Psalm should remind us of how God still cares for his people today. It is an encouraging reminder that God is faithful to his people, even when we stray from the flock (see Astounding Truth #10).

Psalm 23 is only six verses long. The sixth and final verse is what makes this psalm so hopeful. This grand finale of Psalm 23 states, "Surely goodness and mercy shall follow me all the days of my life; And I will dwell in the house of the Lord Forever." This means that those who know Christ are guaranteed a never-ending relationship.

Unlike our relationships on earth where people come and go into our lives, God will never abandon us. He will not leave us, regardless of how difficult, emotional, or wayward we become. He will chase us every moment, every day until we comprehend the vastness of his faithfulness. His "goodness" and "mercy" are two astounding character traits that God has revealed to David through the highs and lows of David's life, which are written with transparency in the Psalms. God reveals those character traits to us when we seek him through the challenges of daily life, just as David did as he navigated the peaks and valleys of life.

Lord, Thank You for Your promise to never leave Your people. Help me remember to look for ways You reveal Your goodness and mercy. Allow me the grace to have a heart like David, who spoke honestly about his journey through the highs and lows of living a God-honoring life. Amen.

God Wants Relationship Over Religion

For you are like whitewashed tombs which indeed appear beautiful outwardly, but inside are full of dead men's bones and all uncleanness.
—*MATTHEW 23:27*

Every year without fail, October comes around and we are bombarded with images of dead bones. I find bones to be interesting, but not because of Halloween. My interest in the skeletal system was piqued after the regrettable roller skating accident my mom endured that snapped her radius and ulna. The orthopedic surgeon made an impression on me and inspired my topic for my sixth grade career project at Brownell Middle School. I needed all the details on bones—dead or alive—to quench my curiosity.

I was riveted by the topic of bones long before I knew that the Bible contains forty-five verses about them. While the Lord did not lead me to the orthopedic career I desired as a preteen, He led me to study the verses in His Word that discuss bones and how Jesus used a humerus metaphor to describe how some people related to Him.

At the time Jesus lived, his primary adversaries were the Pharisees. They were the know-it-all types who were fundamental in their pursuits and prioritized the "works" part of the faith, rather than the "faith" part of the faith. Matthew 23:27 shows us just how disgusted Jesus is with His supposed leaders when we read about a lengthy list of woes that Christ uses to characterize the Pharisees. The Pharisees seemed like righteous people on the outside, but inside carried wicked motives. This statement gives a glimpse of how much Jesus detested legalism. Legalism is not a biblical term; however, the principles are clearly outlined in the Bible. To understand legalism, think about obedience to a set of rules, but missing the main point as to *why* obedience to those rules is relevant.

This passage makes sense when you understand tombs in ancient Israel. Tombs were cut out of sandstone and painted white, so they looked beautiful on the outside. However, regardless of how lovely the tombs looked on the outside, they still housed a dead and decaying body on the inside. A body would be left for one year after death. After that time, the tomb would be reopened, and the remains collected and transferred to a smaller box. This is precisely how Jesus described these legalistic religious leaders who exalted the traditional law above God's grace.

Part of legalism is the belief that someone can earn their way into heaven. In this case, they believed that because they were children of Abraham and continued to be loyal to the Jewish law, they were children of God. What the Pharisees failed to realize was the necessity of having an awareness of their sin. Just like the tombs, the Pharisees seemed like righteous people on the outside, but they had wicked motives inside their hearts. Jesus specifically addressed this concept of being spiritually dead in this text. The underlying message is repentance. Repentance is not just feeling sorry for your sin. Repentance plays a role in your salvation process. When we live in sin, we become a tomb: a symbol of death.

Lord, help me to be aware of my sin. Give me a repentant spirit and a desire to turn away from sin and turn toward You. Reveal to me when I am boastful of my works and remind me that nothing I can do will secure my salvation. Forgive me when I try to replace faith with a set of rules. Direct my mind to Your truth. Amen.

-»»»»‹‹‹‹-

God Keeps His Promises

The Lord has done what he purposed; He has fulfilled His word Which
He commanded in days of old. He has thrown down and has not
pitied, And He has caused an enemy to rejoice over you. He has exalted
the horn of your adversaries.

—*LAMENTATIONS 2:17*

W hen a friend shared with me that she met the perfect guy online
(accomplished, funny, good looking, lived in a gated community, etc.),
my skepticism roused. Turns out, this guy's description was misleading. The
"accomplished" adjective described his colorful criminal record and the "gated
residence" meant prison. While I admired his efforts to embellish his qualities
and capitalize on the positive attributes he had going for him in this season, it
was evident that this was not the suitor for my friend.

Unlike the guy looking for love while in lockup, God will never present His
people with misleading words. Every word God speaks is true. His words are
never wasted. "The Lord has done what He purposed; He has fulfilled His word."
(Lam. 2:17) This means you can trust the Bible because it is the written word
of God and the foundation for everything. His Word tells us that every word of
scripture is "breathed out" by God and is true. God divinely inspired all writers
of the Bible by the Holy Spirit.

The Bible is not just a book of wise and notable people who wrote things
down thousands of years ago. The Bible is true (John 17:17). The Bible will last

(Matt. 24:35). And the Bible will not change (Heb. 13:8). It is important to note that religion will change; churches will change; institutions will change; religious leaders will change; authors will change—*But God will never change.* His Word is living and active and powerful (Heb. 4:12). The Greek translation means the Word of God is alive. Not only is God's Word alive, but it also produces abundant life (John 10:10).

The Bible is unlike any book written today. It serves as God's personal message to you. It meets you where you are *today.* As you change, the message of God's love and His faithfulness stays consistent through His biblical promises. The adjective "active" that the Bible uses to describe itself means effective, powerful, producing or capable of producing an intended result. That is precisely what God desires to do through His Word. Reading the Bible reshapes us into the person God has intended us to be.

Lord, use Your Word to mold me into the person You want me to be. Allow me to understand the depth of Your faithful promises through the Bible and know that You will never change. Thank you for the opportunity to know You through your Holy Word. Thank you for being a promise keeper. Amen.

Personal Reflection on the Character of God

God is:

Alive, Awesome, Almighty, Alpha, Abba, Abundant, Available, Approachable, Beloved, Benevolent, Bountiful, Compassionate, Counselor, Comforter, Creator, Companion, Caring, Cornerstone, Constant, Deliverer, Divine, Discerning, Everlasting, Eternal, Exalted, Faithful, Forgiving, Glorious, Gracious, Healer, Holy, Helper, High Priest, Incomparable, Intercessor, Infinite, Immutable, Immanuel, Just, Jesus, Jehovah-Jireh, King of Kings, Lord of Lords, Loving, Merciful, Messiah, Mediator, Noble, Omega, Omnipotent, Omniscient, Omnipresent, Prince of Peace, Praiseworthy, Perfecter, Quintessential, Righteous, Redeemer, Rescuer, Savior, Shepherd, Servant, Sovereign, Sustainer, Trustworthy, True, Unchanging, Unshakable, Virtuous, Vast, Wonderful, Xristos, Yahweh, and Zealous

- What characteristics of God do you most appreciate today?
- Who has been the most influential person to model Christ-like character to you?
- What specific steps are you taking to live a life that reflects the character of God?
- Which Astounding Truth has had the most impact on your understanding of the character of God?

PART II

God's Desire for His People

—>>>>>><<<<<<—

The next 25 Astounding Truths are centered around God's desire for His people. The Bible is the foremost way that we learn about God and become familiar with His aspirations for the people who follow Him. Through my study of the Bible, it has become clear that my purpose is to have a relationship with Him. He desires the same for you (see Matt. 11:28).

Our obedience and belief in Him are how we demonstrate our love for Him. This is not through our bloodline, or trying harder, nor through our will (see John 1:13). God chose *you* to know what He desires of you for one reason: because *He loves you*. This is regardless of how busy you are, how distracted you are, how comfortable in life you are, or how afraid you are. He desires your adoration because He created you for His glory. He loved you so much that his goal is to redeem and restore all that sin has destroyed by sending His Son Jesus to die for you (John 3:16).

Part of God's desire in giving us the Bible is so that we can gain an understanding of who Jesus is. Who is Jesus to you? It is an important and necessary question to ask because Jesus asked it 2,000 years ago (see Luke 9:18). The relevance of this question is required to understand the Christian faith. The Bible is God's infallible Word, but sometimes even well-meaning Christians do not know what it says about who Jesus is. The bulk of this section contains New Testament Astounding Truths about who Jesus is and why He left heaven to join His people on earth for a short time. I pray that God speaks to you and meets you through reading this section as He met me through writing it.

God Desires Awe of His Marvelous Works

For You formed my inward parts; You covered me in my mother's womb. I will praise You, for I am fearfully and wonderfully made; Marvelous are Your works, And that my soul knows very well.

—PSALM 139:13–14

There is nothing quite like hearing the news of a new pair of genes. My husband received the news that I had a third baby in utero when I tricked him into thinking our oven was broken. I worked hard to keep a straight face when I interrupted his basketball game with the neighbor kids and asked him to come inside and have a look at our new oven we had just purchased for our home in Bothell, Washington. Upon opening the oven, he discovered a single Kirkland brand bun in the oven. That bun represented our baby girl, Lily, who at the time was only the size of a thimble in my womb. Bryan received my pregnancy announcement with joy and excitement, as well as the relief that our new oven was *not* needing a repair.

The gift of life is extraordinary. King David wrote about his own conception and his time in the womb in Psalm 139. This Psalm is one of the most beloved Psalms because it expresses the infinite knowledge of God and how He was intentional in designing every person. Even with all of our complexities and intricacies, God was intentional in designing us just as He saw fit. This attribute of God is referred to as omniscience. God desires for his people to be completely enamored by His all-powerful (omnipotent), all-knowing (omniscient), and all-present (omnipresent) Spirit. David burst into an expression of praise to God in these verses to emphasize these attributes and remind himself that he should always be in awe of God's design for how he was made.

It is through these Psalms that God also desires that we understand the topic of conception and life is a biblical issue (not a political issue as the world may lead you to think). The Bible is clear that God is the author of life and thus determines when life begins and when life ends (see Gen. 2:7; Acts 17:25; 1 Tim. 6:13; John 1:3) The truth of God's Word in Psalm 139:13–14 is that our lives are not accidents. God made you and because you are made in His image, you have inherent worth. If you have ever struggled with your purpose as David did, this verse was written by God for *you*. Ask God for wisdom in discerning your purpose (James 1:5). He will reveal this to you, on his sovereign timeline. He gives us exactly what we need, at an appropriate time in which He sees fit.

God gave me a tremendous blessing of a literal object lesson for Psalm 139. My fourth baby, Levi, was born with a unique birth defect. An anatomy scan at nineteen weeks gestation revealed he had a cleft lip (not to be confused with the biblical cleft that hid Moses from God in Exod. 33:22). The news of Levi's cleft and the inconclusiveness of the severity was an extremely difficult diagnosis to process. Yet, it forced me to cling to the truth of Psalm 139; that this baby was *fearfully and wonderfully made in His image*. From the moment of conception, his life was known by God. What a refreshing and (more importantly) upgrade from the world's view about visible birth defects. Fast forward to Levi's birth, it was revealed to me that my little cleft cutie was the most visible expression of the Lord's redeeming love and joy for our family, and for my calling as a mother.

Lord, I praise You for creating me in Your image. Thank you for knowing me so well. Help me to remember this when I struggle to find my purpose. Help me to honor you with my life and stand firm in Your promises that You are the author of life. Equip me with an unwavering desire to be bold in the biblical belief that all human life is precious to God. Amen.

-》》》？《《《-

God Desires Marital Harmony

Wives, submit to your own husbands, as is fitting in the Lord.
Husbands, love your wives and do not be bitter toward them.

—*COLOSSIANS 3:18–19*

Upon entering our home on Joe & Flo Drive, you will see a flood of photos of Bryan and me, looking like a living endorsement for marriage. You'll see us on 07/07/07 with me wearing a lace bridal gown accompanied by a Mantilla veil, alongside a cute groom in his dress blue uniform. You'll see a happy couple on a beach, surrounded by four kids in monochromatic hues to match the ocean. You'll see Bryan hugging his wife after a long hike, wearing his prized fanny pack. Ah, if only every moment of marriage was as blissful as those magical moments caught on camera.

Fortunately for us, the Bible offers a recipe for marital harmony. Ironically it was written by Paul, and it is unknown if he had a wife. Paul tells the Ephesian believers that both men and women have a high calling in marriage. To men, Paul writes they should love their wives as Christ loves the church (Eph. 5:25). That command to husbands is restated by Paul in Colossians 3:19; however, this time he adds that husbands should not be bitter toward their wives. I've used the New King James Version of the Bible for this book, but decided to view Colossians 3:19 in other versions. I like how the English Standard Version of the Bible uses the word *harsh*. Husbands love your wives, and *do not be harsh with them*. Regardless of your preferred translation, we can understand the point

Paul is making. He exhorted the early Christian men to treat their wives with compassion, leading them with gentleness and love.

At the time Paul's letter to the Ephesians was written, Greek and Jewish culture heavily influenced the new followers of Christ. In both cultures, men held privileges women did not have. Greek culture dictated that men were superior and Jewish culture dictated that a woman was under her husband's authority. Paul's message was consistent with the message that Jesus brought and challenged current cultural assumptions in a big way. He wanted the new believers to know that men and women are equal in Christ. The same is true today. If you are following Christ, your marriage will look different than what the current culture says about marriage. Current culture says we are to be happy in marriage. Biblical marriage says we are to be holy in marriage. The contrast is astounding.

Jesus modeled loving his church by building her up, modeling patience, praying for her, helping her flourish, and teaching her. What a completely refreshing and encouraging list of commands given by Paul on how husbands should love their wives well. To women, he writes harmony is achieved by lining yourself up with your husband, submitting yourself to your husband, and trusting your husband to care for you. Submit means to voluntarily yield to another, which translates to yielding in such a way that pleases God. My submission to my husband is voluntary, yielding all for God's glory. God desires His people to have a biblical view on marriage that will produce glory and honor for God through obedience to His commands.

Lord, help me to desire Your mindset regarding marriage. Equip me with the tools to promote the biblical commands You have ordained regarding marriage. Help me decipher Your wisdom for marriage and silence the voice of the Enemy and the world's view on marriage. Amen.

-»»»≫⋘⋘-

God Desires Us to Understand the Assignment

Then God blessed them, and God said to them, "Be fruitful and multiply; fill the earth and subdue it; have dominion over the fish of the sea, over the birds of the air, and over every living thing that moves on the earth."

—GENESIS 1:28

She "Understood the Assignment" is a slang term that has become a popular way to praise someone who went above and beyond to do good. *Urban Dictionary* defines it as "someone giving 110%." Will Ferrell was cast to play an innocent and optimistic oversized elf who was full of Christmas cheer every day of the year—Will understood the assignment in his movie, *Elf.* I was called by God to write 100 bite-sized explanations of curious scriptures in simple language—I understood the assignment. Adam and Eve were given a command by God—they understood the assignment. Before we unpack the success of the world's first power couple created by God, we should get a foundation laid, just like Eve did in obedience to God.

The Bible opens with a beautiful narrative of creation, described over a six-day period. Yom is the Hebrew word for "day" used in this text. This word can refer to an extended period, not necessarily a 24-hour period as we understand the word day. We know the creation story took place in a six-day period, but these are separate unknown intervals of time. On Yom six God said, "Let Us make man in Our image" (Gen. 1:26) and followed up with "be fruitful and multiply and fill the earth" (Gen. 1:28b). They understood the assignment, even though sin disrupted God's perfect plan. This assignment was intended to be literal (multiply the population) *and* fill the earth with *image bearers*. As an *image bearer* of God, this means reflecting God's nature and His character to the rest of creation. If you need any guidance on understanding God's character, please go back and reread the first section of this book.

God's command to Adam and Eve to be fruitful and multiply and fill the earth with image bearers stands in direct contrast to the pagan fertility cults, where humans attempted to persuade the gods to be fruitful. In God's kingdom, that model is reversed. God alone is the giver of life. God specified that people were made in His image, after His likeness. God gave humans dominion over earth's living creatures and instruction to subdue the earth, which is instruction to make the earth's resources beneficial to them. The word "subdue" comes from the Hebrew verb *kavash*, which means to place your foot on the neck of your conquered enemy and bring them under complete control, like when training animals to use for farming. God intended us to understand these verses by understanding His desire for us to care for nature and animals.

God speaks the entire dialogue of Genesis Chapter 1, but He uses the word "Us" (let Us make man in our image, verse 26). By using the plural form, He gives us a precursor to the concept of the Holy Trinity. Trinity is not a word found in the Bible, but is a word used to explain the concept of God in three persons— the Father, Son, and Holy Spirit. As bearers of the image of Jesus, God's desire is to promote the message of the kingdom of God. Today, we understand the God-given assignment by embracing His message of filling the earth with image bearers. You can aid in this process by loving people well and giving credit to the Lord Jesus for your ability to model the love of Christ to others. If you are already doing this, then congratulations—*you understood the assignment.*

Lord, help me to heed Your assignment. You've called me to be an ambassador for Your glory. Allow me to have Your understanding of filling the earth with people that unapologetically bear Your image. Equip me to serve in this role for Your glory. Amen.

God Desires His People to Not Live in the Flesh

Now the works of the flesh are evident, which are: adultery, fornication, uncleanness, lewdness, idolatry, sorcery, hatred, contentions, jealousies, outbursts of wrath, selfish ambitions, dissensions, heresies, envy, murders, drunkenness, revelries, and the like; of which I tell you beforehand, just as I told you in time past, that those who practice such things will not inherit the kingdom of God.

—GALATIANS 5:19–21

Before the Bible became my roadmap for success in life, I remember hearing a woman speak of being fleshy and assumed she was referring to her increased level of body fat. I could completely relate, as someone who had birthed four babies and rode the roller coaster of weight gain and loss. I emphasized with her as I felt my own shame of carrying unwanted weight. I confided in her regarding my journey in navigating the struggles of learning the discipline of buttoning up my diet to hit my ambitious goal of achieving twenty-six percent body fat. This woman patiently waited for me to wrap up my mini podcast, so she let me know that her struggle with being "fleshy" was related to her sin of envy.

While being fleshy in the physical sense is a springboard for a variety of health challenges, being fleshly in the spiritual sense is completely contradictory to God's desire for His people. Two words, with different meanings and different spellings. Theologically speaking, the word "fleshly" refers to our sin tendencies. No thanks to Adam and Eve who brought sin into the world, we are all born with a sin nature. The Bible proposes a far better alternative for living in the flesh, and God used the Apostle Paul to be the agent to deliver the critical message on spiritual wellness.

The Apostle Paul founded a series of churches in the Roman providence of Galatia. Years later, some old school religious leaders visited those churches and tried to reintroduce the former ways. They were trying to bring back the regulations of the Mosaic Law (the set of rules that God's people were commanded to live by before Jesus arrived). This made Paul rage. However, his indignation was not in vain. The book of Galatians came as a result of his anger. Paul wrote this letter to the confused people of Galatia, to help them see what the message of the New Covenant was all about. He wrote it plainly: trust in Christ Jesus, not the Law.

Throughout the book we see several reminders of the contrast between flesh and Spirit. Galatians 5:19 kicks off with a litany of sins that are very natural for humans (can you relate?) Paul lists these pleasure-seeking activities in his letter because they were familiar to his audience. His goal in writing this letter was to educate the Galatians on behaviors that followers of Christ should avoid. Fortunately for us, the same wisdom applies to us today, even if we're not reading this letter in Galatia (modern day Turkey).

Whatever city you reside in, this letter is for you. Paul wants us to know that loveless cheap sex, accumulation of mental and emotional garbage, trinket gods, magic-show religions, cutthroat competition, brutal tempers, and uncontrollable addictions are to be avoided. Thankfully, Paul immediately proposed a genius solution. A long list of verbs (known as Fruits of the Spirit) follows the sin litany, beginning in Galatians 5:22. This "fruit" (love, joy, peace, longsuffering, kindness, goodness, faithfulness, gentleness, and self-control) is a comprehensive list of traits that describe the conduct of the way the Galatian church members should be acting. God desires those same fruits for you.

Lord, by the power of your Holy Spirit, allow me to steer clear of the fleshly tendencies that I am wired to desire. Give me a yearning to live a Spirit-centered life. Help me heed Your warning against fleshly desires so that I may live for Your glory. Equip me with love, joy, peace, patience, kindness, goodness, faithfulness, gentleness, and self-control. Amen.

God Desires the Role of CEO

Commit your works to the Lord, And your thoughts will be established.
—PROVERBS 16:3

I was accomplished in my career. My successful real estate sales boosted my net worth. My book sold so many copies the printing company could not keep up with the demand (Lord willing!) All this achievement I have been blessed with is incredible—but I am not the CEO, the broker, or even the author. God is. My life belongs to God and all my successes are credited to Him.

Although I certainly have plans, dreams, and aspirations of my own, the only reason my life has turned out so unbelievably blessed is because the Lord has ordained it. His plans are far better than my plans. Contrary to popular belief, when I prosper, it is the Lord who has allowed the gains, not me. I am simply working, managing the portfolio and the resources He has given me, and writing the book for Him. All my success in life is credited to Him because He has used me for His glory. Before I had a relationship with the Lord, I had a narcissistic voice in the back of my mind often reminding me that my accomplishments are because of *me.*

The biblical world view squelches that self-focused mindset. This means that our business plans, financial decisions, and plans to provide for ourselves should be submitted to the Lord, as stated in Proverbs 16:3. When you honestly commit your decisions and activities to the Lord, it means your will is in submission to His will. When this happens, your plans will be achieved because you are inviting His will to be done "on earth as it is in heaven" (see Astounding Truth #44). When you put God in charge and elevate Him to the position of CEO and commit your actions to Him, the Bible tells us that you will succeed. However, this means success according to God, not necessarily how you measure success.

When God leads, we are forced to stay humble. Knowing that the Lord allows our success is crucial in the life of a Christ follower. "By humility and fear of the Lord are riches and honor and life" (Prov. 22:4). This verse means that the one who lives in fear of the Lord will be blessed by Him. Honoring God and submitting to His authority guarantees that He will bless you as He sees fit. In the story of your life, God is the author. His desire is that you quit trying to steal the pen and let Him write your success story.

Lord, help me remember that my best chance for earthly success is when my plans align with Truth. Allow me to fully trust You, Lord, and not lean on my own understanding (Prov. 3:5). Help me to acknowledge You in all I do and allow You, Lord, to make my path straight. Bless me with clarity on how to live a life in full submission to Your will. Amen.

-›››››‹‹‹‹-

God Desires His People to Go Fish

Then He said to them, "Follow Me, and I will make you fishers of men."
—MATTHEW 4:19

"**G**o Fish!" Jesus started his public ministry with the same message I heard as a kid playing cards with my sisters. I was oh-fish-ially hooked on that game and enjoyed card games as a fun form of entertainment in our cable-free home. I still love to fish; however, now my favorite form of fishing is fishing for compliments from my husband. He loves my highly so-fish-ticated and chic at home uniform, which on most days looks like varying levels of mom grunge. Nevertheless, I fish often, because Jesus desires His people to go fish.

The Bible documents three separate occasions where Jesus tells His followers to "go fish." The first was recorded by Levi (renamed Matthew), the Jewish tax collector in Matthew 4:19. The second was recorded by Mark the Evangelist in his gospel (Mark 1:17). And finally, to reel in the point, the gentile doctor, Luke, records this command (Luke 5:10). However, the command from Jesus is not the same type of fishing I enjoy: collecting compliments. When Jesus said *go fish*, he meant fish for people.

The message of Jesus shared on the Sea of Galilee on the day he called Simon Peter, James, and John is the same message he desires for us today: to surrender and trust. This story provides an example of how God delights in using ordinary people to build His church. The people He selected were typical fishermen, who all had a willingness to obey.

Peter was mending his nets as Jesus spoke to an intrigued crowd of people gathered to hear His message. We know from the scriptures that Peter was worn out, worried, and exhausted from a long night of fishing. Doubtful that Peter would find success filling his mended nets, he willingly gave another attempt after Jesus asked him to try again. The text tells us that as a result of Peter's immediate obedience, so many fish were caught that the net began to break (Luke 5:6). Simon Peter and his team were astonished. Jesus responded to their shock with a simple message that can be summed up in a few words: follow me, from now on you will fish for people. At that moment, the men left everything to follow Jesus.

What God asks us to do will often transcend human understanding. Just like the first disciples, we must be willing participants, commit to a life of following Christ, and submit to Him as our co-Captain. Jesus is the master caster and his public ministry started and ended with the simple message: *Go Fish.* His desire is the same for us today. Submission to His ultimate authority will yield a life of obedience. Obedience to His command to fish for people means go where the people are and offer them the message of hope through Christ Jesus.

Lord, I desire a heart of true surrender to Your will. Help me be bold to go where the fish are, get my hands dirty, and show people Your glory. Use my ordinary life to build Your Kingdom, just as you did for the original disciples of Jesus on the Sea of Galilee. Allow me Your success to build Your kingdom through my fishing excursions. Amen.

God Desires Kingdom Influencers

Now when Athaliah the mother of Ahaziah saw that her son was
dead, she arose and destroyed all the royal heirs of the house of Judah
—2 CHRONICLES 22:10

We have all probably heard the old saying, "The apple doesn't fall far from the tree." This adage states an observable fact that kids usually mirror the unfortunate traits of their parents. I know a few things about apple trees after living in the town of Winchester, Virginia. Much of my parenting journey took place in this town, which is affectionately known as the Apple Capital of the United States. However, unlike the flat plots of land that grow apples in Winchester, in my fantasy fruit orchard, my tree sits atop a high hill and the apples that represent my sinful character traits roll far away from the tree.

The aforementioned phrase is an appropriate phrase for Queen Jezebel (see Astounding Truth #51) and her vile daughter. This Jezebel 2.0, named Athaliah (pronounced "ath-uh-LIE-uh"), shared the same DNA as well as the same aspirations to lead with cruelty. Both women in this mother-daughter duo lived in a perpetual state of anger and were power-hungry idol worshipers. Nevertheless, God is faithful, and He provided critical details regarding Athaliah's reign that serve as a powerful model to indicate how *not to* lead in a position of influence.

Just like her evil parents, Athaliah married for political maneuvering. The Bible tells us her husband, King Jehoram, listened to the wicked influence of others and turned away from God. Athaliah is also credited with influencing her son into a life of debauchery. When her son died, Athaliah found herself on a mission to destroy "all the royal heirs of the house of Judah" (2 Chron. 22:10). She was a woman with an evil plan to destroy the entire lineage of the promised Messiah. To accomplish this, that meant Athaliah had to kill her own grandchildren. *Say what?* (Thankfully the Bible offers a model of a loving and God-fearing Grandma, see Astounding Truth #88).

Like her mother, Athaliah had one goal—to be the first (and last) ruler of the nation of Israel. She attempted to accomplish this by going about it very unconventionally. Typically, kingdom rulers come to power by birth, marriage, or motherhood. Her plan was to completely remove *all* competition. By God's grace, her plot to kill her grandbaby was unsuccessful. Just like baby Moses, baby Joash was spared from death and became king of Judah at seven years old. The hero in this story is his Auntie Jehosheba, who hid him for six years while his evil Granny reigned over the land.

Athaliah completely missed the opportunity to have a godly influence over many in her life through her position of power, beginning with her husband, who she influenced to worship false gods. Secondly, over her son, who she could have influenced by speaking Truth into his life and serving as a positive role model. Her life is not an example of what God intends for those He has called into positions of authority. God desires influencers who are in the business of promoting the message of His authority through those He ordains in positions of influence.

Lord, grant me the insight to follow leaders who are rooted in Your Kingdom. Allow me to see with clarity evil schemes of leaders who have an agenda that is not God honoring. Bless me with Your wisdom in the opportunities You've called me into where I get to have an opportunity to lead others. Let me be an influencer for You. Amen.

God Desires an Awareness of His Political System

And there was a division among them.

—JOHN 9:16

It has been said that politicians and diapers have one thing in common—they should both be changed regularly and for the same reason. Given the brokenness of the modern political system, perhaps a sense of humor is necessary for anyone who attempts to understand the current geopolitical environment. Regardless of how you vote, how you feel about gun policy, climate change, immigration rights, vaccine mandates, government education, foreign policy, same-sex marriage benefits, the economy, role of government, abortion, global trade, crime, terrorism, budget deficit, or any other divisive topic that will reveal itself in years to come—it is critical that we understand that polarizing political views are not unique to modern times.

Like today, the political climate Jesus lived in was particularly unique. He lived and ministered among God's people who were under godless Roman rulers. The Bible also tells us that Jesus engaged with leaders who were the religious elite, but lived as if they did not know God. The gap between these two ways of thinking was wide, yet Jesus came with a distinct mission: to announce the truth of who He was and why He came. This truth was extremely divisive after the Lord's resurrection. And, just like the lengthy list of political contentions listed, truth proves to be alienating today.

We see a snapshot of the division Jesus created in John 9. To understand this text, it is important to understand the limited way of thinking the religious leaders (known as Pharisees) had at the time Jesus lived. These Pharisees had built a wall around their limited understanding of why Jesus came to live on earth. Much like the wall proposed to be constructed on the southern border of the United States as an immigration solution, this metaphoric wall caused conflict and division. John 9:16 sums up the essence of the conflict stating, "there was a division among them." This response came as a result of Jesus performing a miracle on His intended day off (known as Sabbath). Instead of voicing gratitude for the supernatural work of God's grace and for performing a miracle to restore the vision of a man who had been blind since birth, the Pharisees began to quibble about the healing because it was performed on the Sabbath. The fourth commandment mandates God's people to honor the Sabbath by abstaining from all work. Seeing Jesus perform the actions involved to heal the man (spitting, applying mud, and washing) threw the men into a swivet.

The political system of modern times presents a new set of challenges. However, like in Jesus' day, the problem cannot be solved by any particular political or religious party. Paul reminds the people of Ephesus "for we do not wrestle against flesh and blood, but against principalities, against powers, against the rulers of the darkness of this age, against spiritual hosts of wickedness in the heavenly places" (Eph. 6:12). Translation: Satan has his own political system, and it stands in opposition to Christ. The devil's power has influenced many people to become enemies of the ways of God. However, our citizenship in heaven should highly influence the democratic process. Followers of Christ should vote for people who will promote liberty, protect our rights to practice our faith, and live in alignment with Christ.

Lord, bless and guide all political leaders. May they walk in humility and integrity, realizing the responsibility they have and the opportunity they have been given to influence others for Your glory. Draw our elected political leaders to You as they lead and make decisions. Allow Your Holy Spirit to give them clarity and wisdom. Amen.

God Desires Peace for His People

Oh, that you had heeded My commandments! Then your peace would
have been like a river, And your righteousness like the waves of the sea.
—ISAIAH 48:18

T hanks to the modern feminist movement, some women fall prey to wrestling with discontentment in the calling of homemaking. It's me: I'm *some women.* I have fallen into the idea that pursuits outside the home will increase my self-worth. Through this experience, I have learned that asking God for peace through my seasons of discontentment has allowed me to have a kingdom mindset regarding my calling as a homemaker and mom to all the kids He has blessed me with. God has asked me to worship Him through my service to our home and to my family. Make no mistake; this does not mean I am to worship our home and family, as the world has misunderstood this command. I worship God through my obedience to serve the people He has blessed me to care for in this season. His desire is that I have peace in the calling He has placed on my life.

Horatio Spafford is a man who knew something about discontentment. When he wrote a poem in 1873 that later became the hymn "It Is Well With My Soul" he did not write it from a place of peace. Nevertheless, the lyrics begin with "When peace like a river attendeth my way; When sorrows like sea-billows roll; Whatever my lot, Thou has taught me to say, It is well, it is well with my soul." These words were written after the cataclysmic events that lead to the death of his four young daughters as they crossed the Atlantic Ocean via passenger ship.

The opening words of this hymn were not original thoughts. While Spafford made his living practicing law in Chicago, he also served his church as a Sunday School teacher. The phrase "peace like a river" were originally the words of the prophet Isaiah. Isaiah writes of God scolding his people for claiming to know Him, without actually knowing Him. The circumstances surrounding this reprimand led to captivity by the Babylonian army. God essentially said, "all this mess could have been avoided if you remained faithful to me." He desires His people to remain steadfast in their pursuits of Him, even through the storms of life. The people of my island home know something about the storms of life after experiencing the devastating destruction of Typhoon Mawar in May 2023. The days following this category five storm were horrific, yet I witnessed miracles as people remained faithful to the One who has control over everything.

Peace like a river is a poetic way of referring to peace that surpasses all understanding. Peace that comes from close unity in Christ. In the circumstances surrounding the Spafford family hardships, it was evident that the loss they experienced triggered pain and suffering. However, Spafford knew the experience did not compare with the glory that is to come from living a life with God as the Captain.

Lord, I need Your peace to soothe my heart and mind. Allow me to experience peace like a river in my seasons of discontentment. Thank you for the opportunity I have to lay my burdens on you today. Guide my thoughts to be thoughts of Your peace and allow me to have clarity in the calling you have placed on my life. Help me discern the peace of the world from the peace of Christ. Amen.

God Desires His People Be Like a Lily

"So why do you worry about clothing? Consider the lilies of the field, how they grow: they neither toil nor spin."

—*MATTHEW 6:28*

My daughter, Lily, is like the beautiful flower that inspired her name. She possesses a sweet and innocent beauty. Her tenderheartedness is her most enduring character trait. Like the Lily flower, she blooms best when nurtured with compassionate care. She prefers the sun and needs to be well hydrated to thrive. We chose her name before we knew how closely her character traits would align with the flower.

Jesus chose the lily as an object lesson to share some crucial buds of wisdom to His followers. His bold and definitive statements can be found in Matthew 6, following his instructions on how to pray. After the memorable words known as the Lord's Prayer, He ends his sermon with instruction on how to seek the Kingdom of God.

The command to *be like a lily* tops the chart as a showstopper when fear, anxiety, and unrest creep into the mind of a believer. In the most challenging times of unrest, God faithfully reminds us to "consider the lilies of the field," as they grow naturally in the district of Galilee where Jesus did his best teaching. He used these beautiful flowers as an object lesson to help show His followers to trust in the providence of God and use worship as an antidote to worry. He said these words as a reminder to live free from anxiety because we have a Father in heaven who feeds the birds, takes care of the lilies, and provides in all circumstances as He sees fit. He tells his followers that everything they need will be given in order to do His will and that He will supply everything they need to live accordingly.

Worry is a mental preoccupation with something, but God is always sovereign over our worries. He commands us to submit our prayers and concerns to Him. He tells us to worship instead of worry. This is a daily (sometimes hourly) discipline. By the power of the Holy Spirit, who lives in every believer, we can choose to rely on the power of God to live with the challenges that the Lord ordains in our lives. Jesus promises that "in this world you will have tribulation" (John 16:33). God is our creator, provider, and healer; He provides a way for us to not be chained down by our concerns, but to enjoy freedom given to us by the death of His son on the cross. God's desire for His people is that we keep our eyes focused on Him. Worrying puts focus on the wrong object. Recognizing that God has a wonderful plan for your life can help you to remain faithful during seasons of unrest.

Lord, help me to abide in You when anxiety and worry take over my mind. I trust that You have provided all I need in my circumstances, to live according to Your will. Grant me peace of mind to walk the path You have laid out for me. Help me remember Your command to be like a lily when my flesh causes me to get stressed over things I cannot control. Amen.

God Desires That His People Be Blameless Before Him

But you must be blameless before the Lord your God. The nations you are about to displace consult sorcerers and fortune-tellers, but the Lord your God forbids you to do such things.

—DEUTERONOMY 18:13–14, NLT

It was 1994. The latest free issue of *Seventeen* magazine arrived. Happiness abounded when the horoscope page told me my crush and I were completely compatible. Our signs were perfect, and all the stars aligned for a beautiful life together. As a teenager, it was easy to be attracted to the colorful and well-designed presentation of information printed by this successful magazine. It was also easy to get sucked into the mindset of reading horoscopes to gain insights into my character and get a snapshot into my future romantic life.

Horoscopes are determined by astrology and people who rely on them believe that planets and stars determine the path for life. However, the Bible presents a contrary view on this topic. Astrology, crystals, tarot cards, palm reading, and anything remotely related to this list opposes Biblical teaching because it advocates faith in something other than the Lord.

The Bible records that Moses had difficulty speaking (see Astounding Truth #90). However, he had a lot to say on this topic. Deuteronomy 18 begins with teaching on true worship but takes a sharp turn beginning in verse 9 when Moses warns about avoiding wicked customs. He speaks of the various demonically inspired customs of nations intending to manipulate false gods to act in favor of the person seeking help. He speaks on divination, which is an attempt to gain secret knowledge by interpreting omens or looking at astrology. Moses was relentless on this topic, trusting that God gave him a platform to teach truth to His people. He transitions into a discussion of sorcery and spells. Moses spoke of witchcraft, by which people attempted to gain insights into the spiritual realm. As if that list is not comprehensive enough for seekers of the occult, Moses lands the plane by addressing spiritism. Contacting the dead, holding seances, and playing with Ouija boards are current forms of spiritism and should be avoided by people of God.

God commands us to be *blameless* before Him by not following the ways of the world. Instead, God provides a solution for gaining divine knowledge in the verses that follow. Moses wrote that God would provide prophets (Deut. 18:18) to bring His word to his people. He confidently assured them that they did not need to follow the ways of the Canaanite people who were popular influencers at the time Deuteronomy was written. A succession of prophets would follow to deliver Truth to God's people. God assured His people that He would "put my words in their mouth." The Truth of this message remains the same today. No need to seek false information to gain insights into your opportunities to prosper. God will reveal Truth to you when you seek Him.

Lord, let me not be easily swayed by the message of the occult. Allow me to be bold in my knowledge of Your Word when the world seeks to influence people by any means that are counter to Christianity. I ask for God's light to shine Truth to those who are involved in these practices of sin. Amen.

God Desires That We Stay In Our Lane

But we urge you brethren, that you increase more and more; that you also aspire to lead a quiet life, to mind your own business, and to work with your hands, as we commanded you.
—1 THESSALONIANS 4:10–11

Marine Corps Drive is the main thoroughfare on the island of Guam. This twenty-one-mile highway runs from the main gate of Naval Base Guam directly to the main gate of Andersen Air Force Base. Cruising this road will allow you to see tropical forests, urbanized commercial areas, and residential neighborhoods with carabao (domestic swamp-type water buffalo which serve as Guam's unofficial national animal) feasting on local brush. In the section closest to where I live, the seven-lane oceanfront highway provides easy access to all Hagåtña has to offer. Like most capital cities, navigating through town is easiest when you know which lane you need to be in.

The apostle Paul wrote a letter to the people of Thessalonica to drive the point home about staying in your lane, much like navigating an unfamiliar city. He commands his audience to lead a quiet and peaceful life, to mind their business, and to be industrious. This instruction was given to the Thessalonian church by Paul to encourage the young believers to have order in their lives. His desire in writing these words was simple—to help the followers of Christ have accountability for their actions. He wanted to encourage people to have an authentic and honorable walk with Jesus. As followers of Christ, we are *not* to stir up trouble. When Paul wrote this letter, his concern was rooted in the simple message that Christians should live peaceful lives.

Paul wrote a direct challenge to the people—to work with their hands (verse 11). Evidently, some of the Thessalonian believers became so overzealous about the return of Christ that they quit their jobs. Somehow, they thought that while waiting on Jesus, they did not have to work. Thankfully, Paul gently instructed them to get back to work.

It has been almost two thousand years since this letter was written and we are *still* waiting for Christ's Return. Paul's words also reminded people that while waiting for Jesus, we are not to drain the resources of the Church body. Christians are not to be lazy. Until Jesus returns, we are commanded to work as if God is our direct supervisor (see Astounding Truth #95) and to honor God with our talents and abilities. Any kind of work we do can be spiritual work, if it is done to God's glory. The Bible provides many examples of people who worked to glorify God with their artistic abilities using their hands. Never underestimate your industrious and artistic talents to be used to bless others in the faith and to honor God by using the skills He has given you.

Lord, I praise You today for the talents you have blessed me with. Allow me the desire to use my industrious and creative skills for Your glory. As Paul encouraged the early church, equip me with a desire to live a quiet life and mind my business. Thank you today for the encouragement You give regarding my attitude toward work. Amen.

-»»»«««-

God Desires That His People Be Like a Wall

If she is a wall, We will build upon her a battlement of silver; And if she is a door, we will enclose her with boards of cedar.

—SONG OF SOLOMON 8:9

"When one door closes, another door opens," is a commonly heard slogan of encouragement when life's path does not align with what was hoped for. After I completed sixteen interviews for various graduate schools across the United States, I had my heart set on a small Catholic school in Iowa. This was the path I wanted, but they woefully did not want me. Fortunately, another door opened and led me to accept an opportunity at North Carolina State University which redirected my life's course in the best possible way. Turns out, a Midwestern girl could fit in quite well in Dixieland, despite the fact that I did not own anything monogrammed, a cashmere sweater, a gingham dress, or a strand of pearls.

The biblical door reference was originally spoken by King Solomon in the mid-tenth century B.C. referring to promiscuity. God gave the important task of writing about licentiousness and virginity to King Solomon, even though he deviated significantly from the biblical ideal for marriage. He had upwards of 1,000 wives and concubines (a woman who lives with a man but holds a lower status than a wife). Solomon used poetic and metaphorical language throughout the entire book of Song of Songs to describe courtship, a wedding day, romance, risks with love, and purity.

The 22nd book of the Bible is translated from Hebrew as "Song of Songs," which is like saying "The Very Best Song." The book also boasts the title of "Song of Solomon" referencing the author. At first glance, the overarching theme of this book is human love and sex. However, the Astounding Truth that is revealed through these poetic verses is that Solomon wrote these words to teach us about love and sex redeemed. Through these words, we are reminded of how different human love looked before sin entered the world. Solomon shows us that love and sex are not inherently evil, rather that they contain the beauty that God intended when He created it. This view is contradictory to the view of the Greek philosophers, who had a competing perspective at the time this book was written. Homosexuality was encouraged, pederasty was acceptable, and prostitution was legal in ancient Greece.

Solomon used a construction metaphor to teach the reader there are two kinds of women. The loose woman is a door (more about her can be found in Proverbs 7). The wall refers to the pure, kingdom minded woman. These building metaphors were used by a group of brothers considering how to best prepare their young sister for marriage. We know she is young because the text tells us she has no breasts (Song of Sol. 8:8). Let this text serve as inspiration for discussions among family members. Teach your little sister, daughter, and niece that they should be like a wall, having enough self-respect to resist the modern feminist movement and cultural pressures to conform to the way the world promotes females to live.

Lord, I thank you that Your word provides instruction on dating and marriage that is designed to honor You. Allow my relationship to give glory to You. Equip me with a desire to be like a wall as King Solomon had advised. Like the Shalamite's brothers, help me teach Your Truth to young women in preparation for marriage. Amen.

God Desires That We Turn the World Upside Down

"These who have turned the world upside down have come here too."
—*ACTS 17:6*

Lifestyle Influencer seems to be a growing career opportunity for people who have talent with a selfie stick and are comfortable sharing the noteworthy and mundane details of their lives. Social media marketing thrives when successful influencers promote products and services, guiding the actions of the people who "follow" them in a particular way. Currently, my favorite influencers are those who have made their platform popular by poking fun at actual influencers. John Crist nailed the influencer spoof when he portrayed the notion of biblical characters serving as modern day lifestyle influencers. I laughed so hard I had tears streaming down my legs when he promoted fruit as a great tool for tempting your husband and cursing humanity forever (see Gen. 3).

Before being an "influencer" became trendy, one dynamic biblical duo created the mold for influencing. The Bible uses the phrase "these who have turned the world upside down" (Acts 17:6) to describe the dramatic effect Paul and Silas had on the people of Thessalonica. Unlike modern times, where the goal of influencer marketing is to affect purchasing decisions, the influence of Paul and Silas had eternal consequences for everyone who had the benefit of receiving the Good News they were called to share. God calls all who trust in the Lord to be influencers as well. Matthew 5:14 says "You are the light of the world. A city set on a hill cannot be hidden." This means your life is on display, for everyone to see—no selfie stick or ring lighting required to make you look more appealing. Followers of Christ are called to influence others by living authentic and exemplary lives, and living in step with the precepts of the Bible.

What does an influencer for Christ look like today? Using the model of Paul and Silas, we can use our voice to encourage believers. When we face difficult challenges like Paul and Silas faced (like going to prison for the faith they were unwilling to denounce) we can remain faithful to God and pray for His favor to be steadfast through the trial. We can serve people with joy and willingness to set aside our comforts for the Gospel. We can travel to places where the Gospel is unknown, to share the Good News of Christ. We can model a fervent prayer life and seek God in all we do. Be encouraged by the example of the original influencer duo. By their testimony, we can live a life God desires for His people who put their faith in Christ.

Lord, let the model of Paul and Silas be an example to me about how to live my faith in a vibrant way. Allow me the opportunity to turn the world upside down to advance Your kingdom. When I am weary, or uncomfortable, or unsure of myself, allow me Your stamina to be bold for the Gospel. Use my skills to influence others to seek You and to understand what You desire for Your people. Amen.

-))))⟩⟨⟨⟨⟨-

God Desires That We Know Salvation Is a Gift

For by grace you have been saved through faith, and that not of yourselves; it is the gift of God, not of works, lest anyone should boast.
—*EPHESIANS 2:8–9*

I was classically trained on the original Nintendo Entertainment System. I received the best gift ever (thanks mom and dad!) on Christmas of 1988 when I ripped the paper off a large box and found the Nintendo game system inside. I don't want to toot my own horn, but (beep, beep) I could save the princess in level 8-4 faster than anyone I knew. It was an awesome gift that provided my sisters and me with many happy moments together. Among other notable gifts, I have also been given the gift of salvation. However, unlike the Nintendo Entertainment System, this gift from God is completely undeserved, gives me eternal security, and it will not break or lose credibility when a more advanced game system is developed. I know this beyond a shadow of a doubt and believe it to be true based on God's Word (Eph. 2:8-9).

In a season overcome by the ordinary experiences of daily life in my faith journey, I prayed a specific prayer one evening: that God would reveal Himself in a fresh new way, and that I would be left in awe of Him and His presence in my life. I needed a personal revival of sorts, and that is precisely what I asked the Lord for.

This prayer I offered was much like the message Paul was trying to communicate with the Ephesian Christians. He wanted them to know how spectacular the gift of God's grace was to them, so he opened Ephesians chapter 2 with a comparison of grace and sin. It is essentially a coroner's report. Paul reminds the Ephesians that everyone outside Jesus is spiritually dead (see Astounding Truth #14). He continues with the reminder that several factors will keep people locked in the coffin—following the ways of the world, Satan, and our fleshly desires are all ways followers of Christ remain dead (Eph. 2:2).

Two words completely redirect the message of Ephesians 2. Verse 4 begins with "But God," and turns the message into a message of hope. Paul tells us that Christ made us alive, saving us by grace. Grace is the unmerited favor of God. It is only available through faith. It is a gift, far better than my Nintendo Entertainment System. God loves and saves us not because of who we are or what we do, but because of the work of Christ. God's presence in our lives is the real present. Be encouraged by the fact that He is working all things for good for those who trust His plan.

Lord, give me eyes to see You, and Your wonderful gift of salvation. Thank You God for sending Your son to die for my sins. Thank you for the amazing grace that saved me. Allow me to be reminded of this Astounding Truth every day and live with the reminder that this gift is Your free gift to me. Amen.

God Desires His People To Pray Without Sneezing

Rejoice always, pray without ceasing, in everything give thanks; for this is the will of God in Christ Jesus for you.
                                        —*1 THESSALONIANS 5:16–18*

P ray without sneezing. It is a Biblical command, at least according to my Grandpa Lucido. The communication snafu occurred when I shared with him the words of the apostle Paul, which serve as my life verse from 1 Thessalonians 5:16–18 "Rejoice always, pray without *ceasing*, in everything give thanks." It brings a smile to my face remembering my ninety-year-old Grandpa laughing with me about sneezing in the Bible. His health was failing, his body slowing down, his ears weak, but nevertheless, he still had a sense of humor.

Paul ends his first letter to the Thessalonians after a long list of exhortations. He is wrapping up his sermon with bite-sized commands, trusting that the Holy Spirit will equip his audience with the knowledge they need to live these commands. The command on prayer looks different depending on which version of the Bible you prefer. Pray continually (New International Version); pray without ceasing (English Standard Version); never stop praying (New Living Translation); pray constantly (Holman Christian Standard Bible). Regardless of your translation, the message is crystal clear. Paul desired to teach us that forming a lifestyle of prayer is the goal we should be striving for as followers of

Christ. Praying nonstop means we are having a continuous dialogue with God, coming boldly to the throne of grace to offer up praise, supplication, intercessions, petitions, and thanksgiving.

Someone who prays continually is someone who does not rely on their own strength (Phil. 4:13). They desire to maintain a close and personal relationship with God by pouring out their heart to God (Ps. 62:8). They acknowledge the Holiness of God (Matt. 6:9). They cast their anxiety on Him, acknowledging that God cares (1 Pet. 5:7). They know that God can sympathize with their weaknesses (Heb. 4:15). They know that God promises that if they ask anything according to His will, He hears them (1 John 5:14). Living a life of continual prayer means a constant conversation with God is happening, and that God is acknowledged as a friend (Ps. 25:14). It also means allowing yourself to praise God for who He is (Dan.2:20).

Lord, your Word tells us to always be in prayer. Give me a desire to have an ongoing dialogue with you, knowing that as I pray Your spirit will guide my words. Allow me to have a deep awareness of Your character and Your faithfulness. Guide my thoughts to be continuously aware of your presence in all circumstances. Amen.

-»»»«««-

God Desires Vision for His People

*But even if our gospel is veiled, it is veiled to those who are perishing,
whose minds the god of this age has blinded, who do not believe, lest
the light of the gospel of the glory of Christ, who is the image of God,
should shine on them.*

—2 CORINTHIANS 4:3–4

I have called in sick to work with an eye problem. That "problem" *eye* am
referring to was that *eye* could not "see" myself coming to work that day. I
used that excuse for missing work before my conversion into the kingdom of
God and becoming a disciple of Christ. Since my conversion, I have learned
that the Bible teaches a remarkable nugget of Truth about eye issues. God is not
timid when speaking of eye problems and spiritual blindness in the Bible. Unlike
physical blindness, which can result from an array of medical conditions such as
diabetes, infections, or trauma to the eye, spiritual blindness is grave because it
results in an inability to see God. Jesus calls unbelievers blind and gives a clear
message to His followers—saving faith is based on seeing.

Paul sheds some light on this topic when he tells the early believers in Corinth
that Satan does everything he can to blind the minds of the unbelievers to keep
them from seeing the light of the gospel (2 Cor. 4:4). He is essentially saying
that those who are lost cannot find the good news of Christ. Paul enlightens the
Corinthian believers that Satan is a strong power over our fallen world. Satan's
schemes will continue until Jesus returns. As a result, unbelievers cannot fully

comprehend the Truth of the Gospel unless God opens their heart and eyes by the power of the Holy Spirit. When you are spiritually blind, you may be able to hear the Truth of the Lord, but you cannot see what it means to be transformed by Him.

Spiritual blindness is tricky and can vary from person to person. For some people, it may look like living an immoral life. For others, it may look like putting themselves above the needs of other people in their circle of influence. It may even look like missing the big picture of salvation through Jesus. When culture embraces things that are contradictory to God's plan for His people, Satan rejoices in that victory.

Spiritually blind people are unable to see the beauty of the Gospel and the Lord's plan for His people. God's desire for His people is to see the Truth that He has presented throughout the entire sixty-six books of the Bible and through His plan of redemption.

Lord, bless me with freedom from every form of blindness. Allow me Your vision to see the world and others from a Kingdom viewpoint. Thank you for the gift of the Holy Spirit who unblinds our eyes to see Your glory. Give spiritual sight to those who are unable to see Your glory. Amen.

-》》》》《《《《-

God Provides Instruction On How to Evangelize

But as we have been approved by God to be entrusted with the gospel,
even so we speak, not as pleasing men, but God who tests our hearts.
—1 THESSALONIANS 2:4

G rowing up in the Detroit metropolitan area, I was familiar with graffiti. The inner city boasts graffiti murals as wide as humanity. People say graffiti is ugly and irresponsible, but only if it's done properly. Proof of that reality is on display everywhere in the Motor City. If you look close enough, you'll sometimes see a scripture reference tagged along the side of a building or train. It is called *evandalism*. Even though it is promoting the gospel, *evandalism* is still a criminal act and punishable by law.

The second chapter of 1 Thessalonians is titled "Paul's Conduct." We can infer from this title that God desires His people to know there is a right way (and a wrong way) to carry out the calling of evangelism when it comes to building disciples.

Evangelism is spreading the Christian gospel by public preaching or personal witness. God used the Apostle Paul as the poster boy for evangelism. He currently holds the record in the Guinness Book of World Records as the most influential evangelist. In 1 Thessalonians, Paul reminds us that evangelism can be done wrong. Incorrect evangelism is done when the gospel is not included. This may look like talking about Jesus, but not emphasizing what He did for us by His death on the cross. This may look like promoting a particular denomination or encouraging church attendance, without including the precepts of the faith. This may even include sharing your personal testimony of how you came to know Christ, minus the ABCs of salvation (Admitting your sin; Belief in Jesus; and Confession of faith in Christ).

When writing to the early followers of Jesus in Thessalonica, Paul emphasized the importance of not pleasing men, but striving only to please God (1 Thess. 2:4). Paul was interested in honoring only one audience member. Since God was Paul's only audience, he was able to say that God is our witness regarding evangelism. This is critical in the testimony of your faith. If you choose to walk with God, then God will testify on your behalf. Seek comfort in knowing that truth!

Paul continued in this text by reminding his audience to be gentle with the gospel, just as a nursing mother cherishes her own children (1 Thess. 2:7). As a mom who breastfed four babies, I can appreciate that reminder when my flesh wants to get rowdy sharing the faith. Paul previously suffered in order to promote the advancement of the gospel. Nevertheless, Paul was at no time motivated by money or self-glory. He wholeheartedly believed that God entrusted the message of Christ to him, and his motives to share the Good News of Christ were pure.

Lord, allow me the same kindness you allowed Paul when it comes to promoting the work of Christ. Let my conduct be gentle, pure, and selfless. There is no hidden agenda in Your message, God. Let me be bold and truthful when it comes to promoting Your glory. Allow the gospel of Your grace to be promoted through my actions and speech. Amen.

God Desires His Name To Be Praised

"Our Father in heaven, Hallowed be Your name. Your kingdom come. Your will be done on earth as it is in heaven."

—MATTHEW 6:9–10

C hristians are often confronted to identify idols in their lives. For me, my name has been an idol. My comforts have become a top concern and an idol. Upholding my reputation is a priority and an idol. Distracting myself with busyness, food, drinks, media, material possessions, and children has become entirely too familiar and at times a form of idolatry. If any of these statements ring true, then congratulations—I empathize with your fleshly sentiments. However, the Word of God teaches that *our name* is not to be worshiped, but *God's name* (Matt. 6:9).

Jesus gave us the perfect prayer template in Matthew 6 called *the Lord's Prayer*. It models brevity, simplicity, and childlike confidence by acknowledging that God is to be glorified and His purposes are to be achieved. The prayer begins with Jesus recognizing the need to honor God's name. "Our Father in heaven, Hallowed be *Your* name. *Your* kingdom come. *Your* will be done." (emphasis mine). Did I read that correctly? Scripture does not say Annie's will be done or (insert name here) will be done. This prayer duplicates the heart of Jesus by showing us that the gospel does not revolve around us. In my season of B.S. (before salvation), when I thought the world revolved around me, my needs, my desires, and my will were of top concern. Thankfully, the Lord in His lovingkindness and graciousness stepped in and gently pointed me to an awareness that the world does not revolve around me. The world actually revolves around God.

The prayer continues with an honest statement in verse 11 by bringing our attention to some of my favorite carbs. Jesus prays "Give us this day our daily bread." According to this teaching, we are to look to God every day for our sustenance and care. He continues, "Forgive us our debts, as we forgive our debtors." This is understood as spiritual debts. The Bible calls spiritual debts sin. We are to forgive others, as God forgives us. "Do not lead us into temptation but deliver us from the evil one," requires that we face the hard facts of life. Satan is smart, and he will deceive you (I felt this everyday as I wrote Astounding Truths). This serves as a reminder to pray that the Lord will prepare you for the temptations that are guaranteed to come your way. The Lord's Prayer ends on a high note that once again glorifies God: "For Yours is the kingdom and the power and the glory forever." I love this verse. It emphasizes that God's authority is ultimately in control for eternity.

Lord, let this prayer serve as a model for how I should worship You above all else. Let me not be so self-consumed in my daily experiences that I forget Who this life is about. Still my mind and my heart to give praise to the One who gave it all. Give me a desire to praise You, Lord, just as Jesus modeled in this prayer. Amen.

God Desires Dressing for Success

Put on the whole armor of God, that you may be able to stand against the wiles of the devil.

—*EPHESIANS 6:11*

S kiing is my favorite wintertime workout. It is also my favorite way to exercise the level of commitment I have to make a statement when it comes to the amount of proper gear needed—long underwear, ski bibs, gloves, neck gaiter, ski boots, wool socks, goggles, a beanie, along with a trendy ski jacket. We have spent an arm and a leg to break an arm (thankfully no leg). A trip to St. Anthony Hospital Emergency Room in Denver, Colorado was proof of that when Mr. Weber and I shared a day on the slopes to celebrate our engagement.

The Apostle Paul used a metaphor describing what it means to belong to Christ in writing of his conversion experience. He instructed the people of Ephesus to "put on Christ," using the image of taking off frayed clothing and putting on a modified and improved version. The new outfit he referred to is called the full armor of God (Eph. 6:13). Just like the long list of ski gear needed for a successful day on the slopes, the six-piece clothing and accessory stockpile called armor is used to dress for success in the Christian life. Notice that Paul emphasizes the full armor, listing items that cover the entire body. Paul reminded us in his letter to not be a spiritual streaker and only put on the helmet. He wrote, *put on the whole armor* described in Ephesians 6: breastplate, belt, shoes, shield, and sword to fight off the attacks of the devil. All pieces are necessary for battle against the enemy.

Although this letter was written to the believers at Ephesus two thousand years ago, the message applies to twenty-first century Christians to remind us that people are *not* our ultimate problem. Our real struggle is not against flesh and blood, but against evil spiritual forces in heaven. This is called spiritual warfare, and was once a topic I considered taboo. As God has grown me in my faith, I now embrace the awareness of what spiritual warfare looks like in my life and how to combat the schemes of the enemy.

The cartoon version of the devil does not do justice to what this sneaky little red guy with horns and a pitchfork actually does. His ultimate goal is to deceive us. The devil is like the opposing sports team that views films of your team. By viewing your previous games, the opposing team knows your shortcomings. By knowing where you are weak and understanding your sin patterns, Satan can deceive you and keep you from experiencing the joy that God has ordained for the life of a Christ follower.

It is essential to realize that your human strength will not work in fighting this battle. Therefore, God tells his followers that we must put on this gear before battle. To wear truth like a belt means to live with authenticity before God. To wear the breastplate of righteousness means that our heart is protected from the enemy. The sandals represent peace. Knowing that the devil is a liar, God's peace will combat his schemes. The remaining battle gear all serve an intended purpose to help us be victorious in Christ.

Lord, when the devil attacks, allow me to be prepared for battle. Call to mind every piece of battle gear needed to fight the enemy and protect my mind against his lies. Open my eyes to the areas of my life that are not pleasing to You. Thank you for the gear you have equipped me with to stand firm against enemy attacks. Comfort me in my moments of spiritual warfare and reveal Your truth to me. Amen.

God Desires That We Model a Biblical Businesswoman

Now a certain woman named Lydia heard us. She was a seller of purple from the city of Thyatira, who worshiped God. The Lord opened her heart to heed the things spoken by Paul.

—*ACTS 16:14*

F *orbes* publishes an annual list of the world's most ambitious female entrepreneurs. They are women who have changed the world with their progressive and pioneering business pursuits. While I am eager to see my name on the next list published by *Forbes* for the entrepreneurial and creative efforts of how *Astounding Truths of the Bible* has changed the world, I'll commit to managing my expectations in the meantime. Until then, I will focus on sharing the story of a Biblical businesswoman who is worthy of this title.

Acts 16:14 describes Lydia, an ambitious and resourceful woman. She had a thriving and successful business as a fabric dealer for the rich people of Philippi. Her luxury textile business was profitable and today she would be called a "seeker" of the faith. Lydia displayed a sincere interest in getting to know the mission of Jesus during the height of her business. It was in that season when she met Paul, a missionary man out to tell everyone about Jesus and His Resurrection. She listened intently as Paul preached and the "Lord opened her heart to heed the things spoken by Paul" (Acts 16:14), which caused her to believe. The following verse tells us that she and her household were eventually baptized, which serves as a biblical model for the order in which these events should take place.

Once her conversion occurred, Lydia was blessed with the spiritual gift of hospitality. Like the women recognized by *Forbes*, Lydia was a wealthy woman who had a home large enough to accommodate Paul's missionary team. Because of Lydia and her gracious hospitality, Paul and his co-workers stayed in her home. With their housing generously provided by Lydia, they could devote all their efforts to telling people about Jesus. Her home eventually became the first church in Philippi (Acts 16:40).

This testimony of Lydia serves as an example about the work God does in the life of someone before they believe. Jesus said, "no one can come to Me unless the Father who sent Me draws him" (John 6:44). Lydia, the first Christian in Europe, believed not because Paul was an exceptional wordsmith, but because God allowed her heart to be open to genuine conversion. Lydia modeled excellence in her faith, just as she did in her business by opening her home as a missionary headquarters for Paul and his team. Here we see that hospitality is not only a bold and generous act, but can be used for winning people to Christ.

Lord, You are Jehovah Jireh, the God who provides for us. Thank you for the provision of my home. Like Lydia, allow me to have the vision to use my residence for winning people to Christ. Allow my home to be a place of love where all who enter feel the peace of Christ. Amen.

God Desires Us to Know Jesus Paid It ALL

Then Jesus said, "Father, forgive them, for they do not know what they do." And they divided His garments and cast lots. And the people stood looking on. But even the rulers with them sneered, saying, "He saved others; let Him save himself if He is the Christ, the chosen of God."
                                                    —LUKE 23:34–35

My life was saved by a blood donor in 2009. If you have said yes to Christ, the same truth applies to you. I know this fact regardless of your health history, traumatic injury, pregnancy hemorrhage, or any other event that would lead to the necessity of an actual blood transfusion. The blood donor who saved my life is Jesus. His blood was shed for the forgiveness of my sins and for the sins of all mankind.

God desires that we understand that His bloody death on the cross was the propitiation for our sins (see Rom. 3:25). Propitiation is a fancy word for the act of gaining the favor of someone. My favorite New Testament story describes the events leading up to that last-minute blood donation that Jesus gave us so we could be washed clean, even in our brokenness (see 1 John 1:7).

The crucifixion of Jesus was God's plan for His son. The plan was orchestrated so that *every human* could have the opportunity to acknowledge that His death on the cross is what gives eternal life for those who believe. Jesus lived a sinless life while on earth. However, this was not the case for the two men who were executed alongside Jesus. Jesus was the middleman, so to speak.

Matthew, Mark, and Luke all tell the same story. As a bonus to the crucifixion story, we gain insights into the heart of God by the actions of the two men killed alongside Jesus. These men were thieves, and under Roman law, robbery was punishable by death. Though these two men committed the same crime, their hearts were completely different in how they responded to the man between them.

Criminal "A" was rebellious and ridiculed Jesus. He hurled insults at the son of God and failed to come to terms with his own sin before he died (Luke 23:39). In contrast, criminal "B" realized his shortcomings and grasped that his eternal destiny was completely connected to who his understanding of Jesus was. In this exchange, Jesus knew that criminal "B" had a complete heart transformation. Even moments before his death, the criminal understood that something was beyond his present trouble and asked Jesus to "remember me when you come into your kingdom" (Luke 23:42).

By giving us this passage, God desires His people to know that while we still have breath in our lungs, it is never too late to repent and believe the message of Jesus. Criminal "B" may have been within minutes of death, accepted Christ, and heard Jesus tell him the most important words of his life, "today you will be with me in paradise" (Luke 23:43). Whether you subscribe to the theology of John Calvin or Jacob Arminius (or you have no idea who they are), let this text encourage you that there is hope in Christ for everyone who has a colorful past. Your sins are forever dead and buried because of the death of Jesus.

Lord, allow me to believe with genuineness and sincerity that Jesus paid it all. Like the repentant sinner alongside Jesus on the cross, open my heart to faith in Christ which leads to salvation. Silence the voice of the enemy who reminds me of my broken past and limits my understanding of the power of the blood of Jesus. Amen.

God Desires Us to Understand His Amazing Grace

When Jesus heard that, He said to them, "Those who are well have no need of a physician, but those who are sick. But go and learn what this means: 'I desire mercy and not sacrifice.' For I did not come to call the righteous, but sinners, to repentance."

—*MATTHEW 9:12–13*

Composer John Newton wrote a hymn in 1772 as a sermon illustration about amazing grace. If he were alive today, I would ask him *What IS so amazing about grace?* Newton certainly understood the answer to this question from personal testimony during a fierce storm he endured while steering a slave ship returning to England in 1748. Fearing for his life, he prayed for deliverance. God heard his prayers. He survived the storm and the aftermath springboarded his path to Christianity and triggered the breakup with his career as a slave trader. God's Amazing Grace led Newton to a new career in ministry.

More answers to the aforementioned question can be found in the Bible where we see various testimonies of how God loves sinners. Beyond that, He wants us to embrace our humanness by knowing and understanding His plan for salvation. At times the concept of grace seems too good to be true. Grace is completely undeserved. But by God's mercy, we have been restored to a right relationship with God, through the death of His son Jesus. Understanding God's grace is easier to understand when we focus on what God is doing in our lives, rather than what we are doing to enhance our efforts to be right with God.

Gospel writer Matthew describes his calling by Jesus in Matthew 9:9–13. This text gives us a snapshot of God's gospel of grace. God used a thriving sinner—a tax collector—to write the first book of the New Testament. Often tax collectors took more money than what was owed to the oppressive Roman government, so naturally they were despised by God's people.

Through the calling of Matthew, we see that Jesus came to reform and enlighten not only the righteous, but *all* people. His first words to Matthew were "follow me" (Matt. 9:9). Without delay, Matthew obeyed. Those who witnessed this preposterous scene asked Jesus, "why do you chill with tax collectors and sinners" (Annie Weber translation). Jesus replied with a succinct answer that knocked the sandals off the religious elite. He said, "It is not the healthy who need a doctor, but the sick." This medical analogy provided clarity to those who heard—Jesus did not come to save the secure: He came for the lost.

Jesus was born, lived a sinless life, and died for tax collectors, teachers, executives, nurses, athletes, housewives, tech gurus, maintenance workers, financial investors, and even addicts, prostitutes, and adult film stars. Understanding this is the entry point for understanding the concept of radical grace. Remembering the scriptures that describe how Jesus treated the outcasts of society, spoke to the lost, and ate meals with them helps us to realize that salvation is attainable for *everyone.*

Lord, Thank You for extending me radical grace in my brokenness. You are merciful in spite of my sin. I ask that You allow me to accept the fact that through Your Son, all my sin is forgotten. Infuse me with a continuous sense of the vastness of your love for me, and my understanding of how sick I was before you revealed Yourself to me. Amen.

-»»»?‹‹‹‹-

God Desires Relationship with Him

He was in the world, and the world was made through Him, and the world did not know Him. He came to His own, and His own did not receive Him.

—JOHN 1:10–11

"Words are the source of misunderstandings." This quote from the children's book *The Little Prince* challenges everything we know about communication theory. Proof of that was revealed when my daughter, Lucy, retold a communication snafu that occurred on her first day of high school. "What lunch do you have?" her friend Cecelia asked. Lucy's reply was swift and confident. With zero hesitation she said, "Sandwich and an apple." I immediately recognized the misunderstanding, and it made me laugh. Her friend was asking what lunch *period* she had, not what *kind* of lunch she had.

Like the misunderstanding regarding the lunch period, a frequent point of misunderstanding I have experienced revolves around the question, "are you religious?" My typical answer is always "no, but I am relational." My response to this question is intentional because Jesus himself, the central figure in the world's largest religion, had some thoughts on "religion." So did His early followers. They did not invite people to join a religion; they modeled an opportunity for others to meet Jesus by coming into a relationship with Him. A similar question that required a dialogue (possibly more dialogue than preferred) was when I was asked to identify my religious preference recently at the Guam Naval Hospital.

The most succinct reply would have been *Christian*, but I wanted the lovely woman who was processing my registration to understand what the religion identified on my medical record involves—so I gave her a mini sermon on what my relationship with Christ looks like.

A relationship with the Lord looks very different from a religion. Relationship involves completely trusting God to sustain and guide your path. Relationship is more than weekly church attendance. A relationship with the Lord means complete surrender to the God, knowing that in this surrender, He will guide your steps in the progressive sanctification process. This relationship with God springboards a complete heart transplant. In this broken world, having a religion or church affiliation can be a point of pride. It can also be a hindrance to your relationship with the Lord. Religion can teach a works-based salvation. Relationship with Christ leads to an awareness that you are justified by grace through faith in Christ alone (see Astounding Truth #40).

Lord, thank you for desiring a relationship with me. Your Word says if I draw near to You, You will draw near to me (James 4:8). I desire that relationship. Allow me to draw near to You through reading and studying of Your Word. Allow me to hear Your voice as I develop a stronger relationship with You. Amen.

God Desires His People to Worship Him

Therefore God also gave them up to uncleanness, in the lusts of their hearts, to dishonor their bodies among themselves, who exchanged the truth of God for the lie, and worshiped and served the creature rather than the Creator, who is blessed forever.

—ROMANS 1:24–25

Thanks to Google, I am up to speed on the rich profusion of sea critters that live in the Indo Pacific waters I have been exposed to since moving to Guam. The vast variety of animals, trees, and flowers I come in contact with on the island are astounding. The smell of fresh plumeria in our yard fills my nose with a giddy rush. The vivid colors of the Parrotfish I have observed while snorkeling are awe-inspiring. The magnitude of the Traveler Palm branches in our neighborhood is impressive. However, as much as I love the landscapes and living things that are included in God's creation, they should never be the object of my adoration. The Bible is clear—we are to worship the Creator, not creation.

Before we unpack Paul's words in Romans 1:25, we need to understand an aspect of sin. Sin is ultimately idolatrous. It is loving something more than loving God. When we worship the gifts of creation but neglect the Giver, we are sinning against God. Paul communicates this message to the people of Rome when writing on the topic. He begins his eloquent letter thanking God for the people of Rome and reminding them that he is praying for them. He encourages them by reminding them that he is not ashamed of the Gospel. All good things, all positive, and all uplifting topics open this letter. However, his letter takes a turn beginning in verse 18. He addresses something that the Roman believers and twenty-first century believers need to hear—that ignoring God will lead you into a downward spiral.

Every aspect of creation that God designed points to Him. By God's grace, I experience this every day as I appreciate the beauty of the island. However, worshiping creation (trees, rocks, animals, fire, sun, moon, stars, etc.) but neglecting the Creator indicates we are participating in idolatry. Moses spoke about being driven to worship creation in Deuteronomy 4:19. He spoke about God being a jealous God in Exodus 20:5 as an indicator that God is offering protection over His people. The Apostle Paul reminds New Covenant believers that the same message applies to followers of Jesus—God alone deserves our worship and adoration above anything that He created.

Lord, my desire is that as I enjoy the beauty of creation, it will ultimately point me to You. Thank you for the wonderful gift of landscapes, trees, animals, and fresh open water. Your creation is wonderful but should never replace the worship I have for You alone. Amen.

Personal Reflection on God's Desires for His People

Inspired by God, through the influence of the Holy Spirit, the Bible is the primary tool we have for understanding what God wants for His followers. Hosea 6:6 says, "For I desire mercy and not sacrifice, and the knowledge of God more than burnt offerings." This means God wants loyalty above sacrifice. We can ensure that we remain loyal to the Lord by letting Him shape the way we live. We can trust in His faithfulness and stand firm in the promises of who He is.

- What is one area of your life where you feel God is desiring you to increase your loyalty to Him?
- Which Astounding Truth regarding God's desires for His people has been the most influential to your faith journey?
- How has the Bible revealed God's desire for you to be more obedient in this season?
- How has your understanding of "relationship" over "religion" shaped your view of God?

PART III

Curious Parts of the Bible

–>>>>)((((–

Part III of *Astounding Truths of the Bible* is where the fun begins! This section was the original vision God gave me when He told me to write Astounding Truths of the Bible. This project began as a children's book with stunning artwork serving as illustrations for the curious and miraculous parts of the Bible (artist TBD). However, because of my inability to keep the text brief to adequately serve my young reader, I transitioned to this devotional style book intended to serve an audience who has graduated from picture books to more sophisticated reading.

Part III of *Astounding Truths of the Bible* is a collection of scriptures that God has included in the Bible that are bizarre, unexplainable, and miraculous. God—who could teach a crash course in creative writing—is ultimately the forerunner of creative writing with His unique style. We gain insights into His kingdom throughout the various writing styles of the Bible. Almost half of the Bible is made up of historical narratives and parables. The remainder is poetry (Psalms), metaphor (Matt. 5:13), hyperbole (Matt. 19:24), idiom (Dan. 5:5), contrast (Eccles. 3) and personification (Prov. 1:20). The aim of these next 25 Astounding Truths is to look at some of the more creative styles of writing used to explain kingdom topics. Some of these are funny, some are misnomers, and some are simply unexplainable miracles intended to amplify our faith in God.

The Original Yo Mama Roast

Now it happened, when Joram saw Jehu, that he said, "Is it peace, Jehu?" So he answered, "What peace, as long as the harlotries of your mother Jezebel and her witchcraft are so many?"

—2 KINGS 9:22

Motherhood is the strangest and scariest hood I have ever been through. It's like a fairy tale in reverse. You start in a beautiful gown on your wedding day and end up in stained clothes cleaning up after everyone. However, the joys of motherhood far outweigh the challenges.

Besides aiding in my sanctification process, motherhood has allowed me to experience side splitting laughter because my son Luke loves to roast his mom. Living with him allows me the privilege of my own comedian who keeps me entertained. How good is God to give me a son who shares my love of yo mama jokes?

Yo mama is so dumb she brought a spoon to the Super Bowl
Yo mama is so stinky she makes Right Guard go left
Yo mama is so ugly even Hello Kitty said goodbye to her

Those are just a few of my favorite yo mama roasts. Another favorite was recorded in 2 Kings 9. In this verse we see Jehu roast Jezebel for being a whore and practicing sorcery, asking, "How can there be peace as long as the idolatry and witchcraft of your mother Jezebel are all around us?" (2 Kings 9:22, NLT).

To modern feminists, Jezebel is probably the most intriguing woman in the Bible. She was known for her strong will, her courage, and her keen awareness of current political knowledge. Those are all great character traits, but when considering names for my baby girls, Jezebel was not going to make my list.

Even thousands of years after Jezebel lived, she still carries her savage reputation. She was the wife of King Ahab, who served as the seventh king of Israel. She used her good qualities to promote evil in her position of influence. Her intelligence was used to concoct evil schemes. She used her boldness to bully and intimidate her people. She used her leadership qualities to control and influence her husband to worship false gods. She used her power as a ruler to do anything she wanted, including murder.

During the season when Jezebel was Queen of Israel, true followers of God despised Baal. (In today's terms, this would be like Christians embracing Satan.) Jezebel is most remembered for fostering the spread of Baal religion. Baal was a fertility god of the Canaanite people, so temple prostitution and loose living were practiced by the Baal followers.

Long before it was culturally acceptable in good humor to roast "Your mom," Jehu made a declaration when he responded to Joram's question of "do you come in peace?" He made his intentions clear by citing the evil sponsored by the king's family. More important than the original *Yo Mama* roast was the unrelenting spirit modeled by Jehu to address the sin of Jezebel.

Let the words of Jehu inspire you when challenged with the question of addressing the sin of others in your circle of influence.

Lord, help me to be aware of my sin when I am tempted to live the values of popular culture. Allow me to see clearly the brokenness of the world, especially when the ways of popular culture collide with Christ. Give me a heart like Jehu to speak into situations when false gods are promoted and sin is elevated by those who do not know you, Lord. Amen.

-꒜꒜꒜꒜꒜-

Our Temporary Housing Situation

*For this world is not our permanent home; we are looking forward
to a home yet to come.*

—*HEBREWS 13:14, NLT*

If I had a dollar for every move I have made since graduating high school, I would be as rich as salted caramel pie. The moves continued at rapid succession in my married life, evident by the fact that all four of my kids were born in different states. The more we move, the more stuff we give away. I now live with an open mind and an awareness that I would rather have a passport full of stamps than a house full of stuff. My family enjoys living like nomads and experiencing different places, cultures, and people. Knowing this, it is not surprising that a frequent conversation in our home is geared around where we should move next.

The Bible gives clarity on the precise location followers of Jesus should ultimately be seeking for their final relocation (Heb. 13:14). The best part about this final move is that no stress is involved with the packing process, and shopping around for the most budget friendly moving company is unnecessary. For those who put their faith in Jesus, the perfect location for their final move has already been determined. We get the joy of looking forward to a home with God in Heaven. This is because every day that ends in *y*, we are homesick for Eden. This means we live in a constant state of nostalgia for the world we were created to live in. This world as we currently experience it is not our home. We were created to live in a perfect and beautiful place with God. Sin came into the world and thwarted that perfect plan. However, the Bible gives us hope with a message that this experience on earth is only temporary, and our final destination is in heaven. My family can rejoice in knowing we have our answer as to where our final move will be, completely in God's timing.

Nothing in our present world will suggest what heaven will be like. The fallen world that we know is only a temporary residence. If you are a follower of Jesus, you must have an awareness that our focus is on eternity. With this perspective, we can more appropriately deal with the difficult circumstances that we face as temporary residents because Jesus himself said "my kingdom is not of this world" (John 18:36).

On this side of eternity, we unfortunately experience feelings of fear, inadequacy, doubts, envy, frustration, anxiety, depression, discouragement and other fleshly emotions that can trap us into thinking and dwelling on our present circumstances. But God, in His grace, has promised that He will rescue us from all of our earthly burdens if we have our eyes peeled on *the home yet to come.*

Lord, Thank You for Your promise of Heaven being the final home for believers and that we are only traveling through this world. Until that time, allow me Your wisdom on living in my temporary home with an eternal mindset. Bless me with Your confidence and boldness to proclaim this message when I experience difficulties in my temporary home. Help me remember that my final destination will bring me Your ultimate peace. Amen.

-»»»»⫸⫷⫷⫷⫷-

Jesus Wasn't So Swole

My servant grew up in the Lord's presence like a tender green shoot,
like a root in dry ground. There was nothing beautiful or majestic
about His appearance, nothing to attract us to him.
—ISAIAH 53:2, NLT

A quick Internet search of all the actors who have played the role of Jesus on the silver screen or television determine one unanimous verdict—they. all. are. easy. on. the. eyes. Men with dark wavy hair, impeccable bone structure, and a lean toned physique seem to be what all casting directors have chosen for the role of our Redeemer. While casting an attractive looking Jesus may do wonders for the film marketing, it may cause some confusion on how the Bible actually describes the physical appearance of Jesus.

The Bible gives a pinpoint description of the physical appearance of Jesus in Isaiah 53. This chapter of the Bible is referred to as "The Suffering Servant" and carries a reputation of causing confusion and arguments among Jewish leaders today. Isaiah prophesies in Chapter 53 that He would be rejected by his people, suffer and die in agony, and that God would see his suffering and death as an atonement for the sins of humanity.

The most astounding aspect of this suffering servant that is contradictory to Hollywood's "ideal Jesus" is found in Isaiah 53:2. This verse reveals the truth about what Jesus will look like. It says that nothing about His appearance will attract us to Him. Nothing about His appearance will cause people to do a double take when He passes by. Imagery in this text suggests that He grew up as a scrawny little seedling in a field that experienced drought. This is not the vibe I get when I see Jim Caviezel play Jesus in *The Passion of the Christ*, Christian Bale in the film *Mary, Mother of Jesus*, or Jonathan Roumie in *The Chosen*.

It is human nature to follow people who have an attractive physical presence, like the movie and TV Jesus. The Bible teaches us that what is attractive in God's kingdom is plain in our eyes. Isaiah communicates through this text that this suffering servant will be looked down upon and passed over. He will know pain firsthand and is "acquainted with deepest grief" (Isa. 53:3). These verses that the prophet Isaiah wrote long before Jesus was born could not be more accurate in describing what Jesus endured while on earth. He was wounded and bruised for our iniquities (Isa. 53:5). And He would die because of our rebellion (Isa. 53:9).

Humans flee from suffering and grief, but we get an understanding from this text that this suffering servant—the Lord Jesus—willingly embraced the suffering He endured for His father's glory. These verses serve as a reminder that followers of Christ do not get to be the judges of beauty. Popular culture suggests that it is common practice to judge beauty; however, the Bible teaches that God sees differently because He looks at the heart, not the outward appearance (for more on the Lord's words on physical beauty, go back and review Astounding Truth #1).

Lord, grant me a Kingdom mindset when it comes to seeing Jesus. Allow me to see Jesus as He truly is. Let me be awestruck by His eternal beauty and willingness to suffer a painful death so I can have an eternal home with God. Captivate my eyes Lord with Your beauty and use me to promote the Truth of who you are to others. Amen.

God Instructs Us to Examine Our Hearts

Anything you eat passes through the stomach and then goes into the sewer. But the words you speak come from the heart—that's what defiles you.

—*MATTHEW 15:17–18, NLT*

I t had been a solid two months since our household goods were packed and shipped from Virginia to Guam. Summer of 2022 brought many changes for our family. We sold our home, gave away everything that wasn't serving us, and relocated to the tiny island of Guam on the other side of the globe. The day our unaccompanied baggage arrived at our new residence on the island was much anticipated. Anxious to get things unpacked, I joyfully opened the boxes. My enthusiasm was met with bewilderment when I got a whiff of something putrid coming from the box. Mission "unpack household goods" could not be thwarted, I had to continue digging until I found the culprit. Turns out, a poopy diaper made its way into our shipment. This stowaway nappy assaulted my senses and gave us all reason to chuckle at the fact that Levi's soiled diaper was so well traveled.

You will find several references to poop in the Bible, most found in the Old Testament. My personal favorite is quoted by Jesus himself when he says, "Do you not yet understand that whatever enters the mouth goes into the stomach and is eliminated?" (Matt. 15:17). This question is direct, succinct, and painfully evident. And it begs the question, why would Jesus state something so obvious?

Matthew's gospel was written to people who were excellent at honoring God with their speech, but their hearts were very distant from God. Because it is the first book of the New Testament, it serves as a bridge between the Old and New. It was written to the Jewish people to assure them that Jesus was the awaited Messiah. Matthew 15 is titled "Jesus Teaches about Inner Purity" and opens with a practical question that was asked of Jesus regarding why his disciples disobeyed the age-old tradition or ceremonial hand washing before they ate.

The 613 rules listed in the Old Testament known as Mosaic Law were established by God for primarily one purpose—to remind God's people to be cleansed and changed spiritually. The process of handwashing when Jesus lived far exceeded the demands of the law. His purpose in discussing food, digestion, and excretion was actually to teach his followers about examining their hearts. He reminded his followers that when they eat, the food goes through the mouth, down to the stomach, and is eliminated. No harm done. He tells them that eating with unwashed hands might make you sick, but it cannot defile you spiritually. It is not about what you swallow that will pollute your life, it is what you vomit up. Jesus wanted His followers to know through this analogy that what comes out of the mouth comes from the heart. This is what defiles a person. The heart is deceitful and where sin begins (Jer. 17:9—see Astounding Truth #77 for more on this topic).

Lord, help me remember the words of Jesus regarding what true defilement is when hate, bitterness, and evil desires are all expressed by my mouth. What comes from my mouth reveals what is in my heart. Give me a new heart so that I may reflect Your glory by my words. Amen.

We Can Learn From a Sandwich

*And it happened, when Israel dwelt in that land, that Reuben went
and lay with Bilhah his father's concubine; and Israel heard about it.*
—*GENESIS 35:22*

The Reuben sandwich is one of the most popular sandwiches ordered at restaurants and hotels in America. I'll take my Reuben with a kosher dill pickle and a side of sweet potato fries. This mouth-watering sandwich boasts the distinctive flavors of sauerkraut, caraway seed, and corned beef. It's a salty explosion of deliciousness on the palate. Back in my carb loving days, this sandwich (along with the French Dip at North Carolina State University) tied for first place in the tournament of sandwiches. The Bible also describes a Reuben, but you will not find me as enthusiastic describing him as I do the sandwich.

Reuben was the firstborn son of Jacob and his wife, Leah. His mama named him Reuben, saying, "Surely my husband will love me now" (Gen. 29:32). The fact that Leah knew her husband's heart belonged to her sister Rachel was the fly in the ointment that caused years of hardship for God's patriarchal family. This ongoing quarrel between the sisters who shared a husband was triggered by their dad, Laban, who is best remembered for putting the "fun" in dysfunctional family (see Astounding Truth #95).

Reuben displayed some good qualities at various times in his life. One honorable mention that demands to be noted is that in the plot to kill Joseph, Reuben was one of the eleven brothers who decided to spare Joseph's life. He voted to throw Joseph into a pit instead of killing him (Gen. 37:24). Reuben also demonstrated love for his father, Jacob, when he offered his two sons as a guarantee for returning Benjamin home safely from Egypt (Gen. 42:37). However, Reuben is most remembered for initiating one major snafu that associates his name with his lack of character—he had sex with his dad's concubine in an effort to challenge his dad's authority (Gen. 35:22). At the time, polygamy was an acceptable way to grow God's kingdom. A concubine was a woman who lived with a man but carried a lower status than a wife. (It is important to note that years later, God was clear in the Law of Moses that polygamy was prohibited, see Deut. 17:17 which states *neither shall he multiply wives for himself.*)

Reuben's sin goes beyond satisfying a lustful appetite. Like the sandwich that leads in popularity, Reuben made a declaration that he was now leading the family by taking his father's concubine. Reuben's purpose to take over leadership responsibilities of the family made the sin he committed even more vile. Essentially, we see that Reuben was impatient to receive his inheritance. We learn eventually in Genesis 49 that because of Reuben's choice, Jacob announced on his deathbed in front of all twelve sons that Reuben removed himself from qualification on carrying the messianic torch. This meant that Reuben would have no opportunity to inherit any prominent position in the family. Some of Jacob's final words before his death reminded Reuben of the gravity of his sexual sin.

Lord, help me to flee from sexual sin. Allow me to remain faithful to Your commands and live a life according to Your will. I ask for the grace to be sensitive to all the devices that the devil will use to thwart Your plan for sexual integrity. I ask for forgiveness for my sexual sin and for Your assistance in making choices that honor my integrity. Amen.

The Futility of a Life Apart From God

But as I looked at everything I had worked so hard to accomplish, it was all so meaningless – like chasing the wind. There was nothing really worthwhile anywhere.

—*ECCLESIASTES 2:11, NLT*

Tropical flowers surrounded me as I said my wedding vows at the Selfridge Air Base Chapel in southeast Michigan. Two days later, Bryan Weber and I began our road trip to Colorado where we would begin our married life. Living in the Mile High City with my new husband was going to be the peak of my life—or so I thought—until three weeks later when news that the US Army needed a certain young lieutenant to aid in a twelve-month mission (in Afghanistan) against terrorism was revealed to me. (Gasp, how dare the military not consider my plans and expectations for my newlywed season?) This news was the biggest buzzkill of my life.

The Bible describes a serious buzzkill in Ecclesiastes 2. This is where we find one of the saddest verses in Scripture. King Solomon opens Chapter 2 boasting of all the great projects and accomplishments he took on (he built houses, planted vineyards, created beautiful parks and gardens, bought slaves, owned livestock, possessed massive amounts of silver and gold, acquired singers, and a harem of ladies) and how he was far greater than anyone else in Jerusalem (Eccles. 2:9). He did not refuse himself *any* pleasure (verse 10). The buzzkill is revealed shortly after this exhaustive list of accomplishments when he admits the sad truth—he is downright depressed and finds everything in life pointless (verse 11).

King Solomon spent his life spending copious amounts of money, investing his energy in pleasure, building his empire, and living in the mindset of "let the good times roll." This party boy learned the hard way that everything in life is futile apart from God. In his wisdom, he realized that the fate of the wise and foolish end up in the same place: the grave (Eccles. 2:15). He hated life (verse 17). He hated the acknowledgement that everything he labored for would end up in the hands of his successor. This led to complete despair (verse 20) and made him question the value of everything he had worked for.

Solomon was forced to come to terms with two difficult questions: Where is God in all this pleasure; can He be trusted to give my life meaning? By the end of the chapter, Solomon comes to terms with the hard reality of life. Ecclesiastes 2:26 states, "for God gives wisdom and knowledge and joy to a man who is good in His sight; but to the sinner He gives the work of gathering and collecting, that he may give to him who is good before God." This reminds us to be looking to God to give our life meaning, even during seasons of depression and despair.

Lord, do not let me live for myself and be consumed with worldly pleasures. Allow me to honor and seek You in my pursuits. Give me joy as I live a life that includes an awareness of Your goodness in all I do. Help me chase you in difficult seasons and remind me just how futile life is apart from You. Amen.

-꒰꒱꒰꒱-

Healing for Itchy Ears

For the time will come when they will not endure sound doctrine, but according to their own desires, because they have itching ears, they will heap up for themselves teachers; and they will turn their ears away from the truth and be turned aside to fables.

—2 TIMOTHY 4:3–4

If the apostle Paul saw the church in America today, we'd be getting a letter. He wrote letters to address the shortcomings of the early church. If he could, no doubt he would carry on the mission of addressing the shortcomings of American Christians.

Paul loved to write letters. He is known for authoring thirteen letters that make up a good chunk of the New Testament of the Bible and redirect false teaching, encourage weary Christians, and preach Truth. In addition to his writing ministry, he spent his time on lengthy mission trips to share the great news of Christ. While traveling on one of his missions, he met Timothy. They eventually developed a mentor/mentee relationship, where Paul took great care in exhorting Timothy to preach the Word with truth.

We'll never know with certainty if Paul needed any soothing relief from a skin ailment, but the context clues indicated that might be the case. Paul used the peculiar word *itching* to reference people who have a fascination with preaching everything *but* the Truth of God. He writes to Timothy:

Preach the word! Be ready in season and out of season. Convince, rebuke, exhort, with all longsuffering and teaching. For the time will come when they will not endure sound doctrine, but according to their own desires, because they have itching ears, they will heap up for themselves teachers; and they will turn their ears away from truth and be turned aside to fables."

—2 Timothy 4:2–4

Unfortunately for Paul, Benadryl was not available to relieve his itching at the time he wrote a letter to his friend, Timothy.

In writing these words to Timothy, Paul clearly wants him to know the truth about the challenges he will face after Paul dies and Timothy takes over. Paul knows that a time will come when people have no stomach for solid teaching. When that time comes, he wants Timothy to know that he will need to remain steadfast in his calling.

Paul is also describing a false teacher in this text. One consistent character trait of false teachers is that they crave popularity and praise from the world. To maintain respect, a false teacher may only teach and preach on aspects of the Bible that are easier for the world to accept. An emphasis on happiness over repentance of sin is an example of preaching only a partial gospel. Paul warned against this because it was common in the first century. It is also common in the twenty-first century.

Paul did not mince words. He wanted people who follow Christ to understand that there is only one standard by which a church is to properly function—the Word of God. This is the Bible, and only the Bible. It is the final authority for all churches. It is the most important authority for teachers of the Word to follow.

Lord, give me a discerning spirit to know false doctrine. Allow me to grow in grace and truth by learning what Your Word says about You. I ask for the wisdom to reject anything that is contrary to the gospel of Christ Jesus. In a world where false teachers can easily be promoted by the Internet, allow me Your wisdom in discerning Biblical Truth. Amen.

-》》》？《《《-

The Blood of Jesus is a Big Deal

For the life of the flesh is in the blood, and I have given it to you upon the altar to make atonement for your souls; for it is the blood that makes atonement for the soul.

—LEVITICUS 17:11

Watching Olympic figure skating as a kid completely prepared me for my ice-skating rendezvous debut. Excited that the ice had just been resurfaced by the Zamboni at the Grand Valley State University all-Greek-mixer, I boldly showed off my ice spinning skills I learned from years of intently viewing winter Olympic heroes. However, unlike Nancy Kerrigan who modeled this skill with excellence at the height of her Olympic career, I landed flat on my face mid-spin. The ice was covered in blood and my plans for a fun night of commingling with the co-eds were redirected to the nearest emergency room in Grand Rapids where the on-call doctor could practice his sewing skills.

Leviticus is the third book of the Bible and like my chin post-injury, it is bloody. Along with instructions for holy living, one of the major themes discussed by the author, Moses, is animal sacrifice. Reading this part of Scripture with a twenty-first century mindset sounds gruesome. However, in ancient times before God sent his Son, Jesus, to die for us, animal sacrifices had to be made to cleanse God's people from their sin. This was because sinful people were not allowed to approach God in the tabernacle without some type of sacrificial offering (see Exodus 25-30 for more clarity on what Mosaic Law teaches about sacrificial offerings).

The concept of animal sacrifice sounds strange to us today. However, it made sense to the Hebrew people because they knew they could not live up to God's requirement for righteousness, so blood had to be shed. This concept of sacrifice presented in Leviticus (like other challenging parts of the Old Testament) points to the pinnacle sacrifice—the Lord Jesus. While the images that come to mind when you think of animal sacrifice are cringeworthy, try to reframe them by asking God to give you an awareness of the drastic effect of sin in your life. We should grieve our sin and rejoice in the fact that the bloody sacrifice of Jesus has allowed us to be completely cleaned up from our sinful ways.

Leviticus presents another relevant message to seekers of the Christian faith who have lived among the world. Living among the world is a metaphor for living life in a way that has no acknowledgement of God. I was twenty-eight years old when God stopped me from living in the world and gave me a new perspective that involved living for Christ. Until that point, I believed that if I lived a commendable life, God would overlook my sin. I had sadly misunderstood the message of the Gospel. Forgiveness of sin comes first, and that is only through the blood of Jesus.

Lord, thank you for the blood of Jesus that cleanses us from all sin. Thank you for allowing me to live on this side of the cross, no longer under the rule of Levitical law. Allow Your Holy Spirit to open my eyes to the redemptive gift of Your blood shed for my sin. While reading scriptures on Mosaic Law, guide me to understand the truth of Your salvation plan through Christ Jesus. Amen.

-》》》》》《《《《-

God Sees Through Phoniness

I know your works, that you are neither cold nor hot. I could wish
you were cold or hot. So then, because you are lukewarm, and neither
cold nor hot, I will vomit you out of My mouth.

—REVELATION 3:15–16

L et's drink about something. Um, I mean think about something. Does a refreshing lukewarm beverage sound like a thirst quencher on a hot day? No thank you—I'll take mine with ice, ice, baby. Nothing quenches my thirst like an icy beverage. On the contrary, in cold winter months, a steamy hot beverage is just what is needed. Drinking hot tea is the quickest way to increase my core temperature after hours spent in the snow. I prefer one extreme or the other, but lukewarm water does not appeal to me because it does not serve either of the intended purposes of hydration.

Jesus used a peculiarly strange adjective to describe the church at Laodicea, the seventh and final first-century church addressed in the book of Revelation. He calls the church members "lukewarm" and follows with "I will vomit you out of My mouth." The imagery creates a less than desirable understanding of how we see our Lord, but nevertheless, the metaphor is used to teach something important about how God views people who ride the fence when it comes to faith.

The analogy used in this text is understood when the reader has an awareness of the water system in Laodicea. With no sufficient water source, Roman aqueducts were used to transport hot water from the hot springs in

Hierapolis and cold water from snow melts in southern Colossae. By the time the water reached the area of the people Jesus was addressing, it was unfortunately lukewarm. The important message communicated to the church was refreshing. He said be invigorating like the cold water in Colossae *or* be medicinally healing like the hot springs in Hierapolis, but do not be unhealthy and undrinkable like the lukewarm water once it arrives on location. The lukewarm water carried no value, just like uninvolved followers of Christ carry no value when it comes to advancing the Kingdom of God.

In addition to the water challenge, the Laodiceans had bigger problems. They thought they were hot stuff in God's eyes. Scripture tells us that they were rich, had an excellent medical school, and were ahead of the times with their progressive clothing industry. However, God saw right through their phoniness and responded directly to the pride this church had by saying to them "you are wretched, miserable, poor, blind, and naked" (Rev. 3:17). This verse exposes the prominent lie of prosperity theology. Prosperity theology (or prosperity gospel) is the belief that material success and financial blessings are the will of God. The Bible shows us that this theology is not accurate. Spiritual corruption cannot be hidden from God. He sees through the disingenuous ways of His people. God's message in Revelation 3 is timeless, relevant, and necessary for advancement of the Gospel today.

Lord, You deserve my full obedience and faith. I pray against the desire to be lukewarm in my relationship with You. Allow me to serve You and promote Your glory with a bold and unabashed passion. Fuel my heart with a hot (or cold!) love for You and keep me humble with regard to boasting in the successes You have ordained for my life. Amen.

Many Foreskins, No Foresight

Then Saul said, "Thus you shall say to David: 'The king does not desire any dowry but one hundred foreskins of the Philistines, to take vengeance on the king's enemies.'" But Saul thought to make David fall by the hand of the Philistines.

—*1 SAMUEL 18:25*

My exposure to the world of true crime fighting is broad thanks to the police ride-along I participated in with my brother-in-law. No one can pull over a speeding Michiganster or a stop-sign disregarder quite like he can. He is the quintessential model public servant, serving with a sense of law and ethics. That experience, combined with twenty-five seasons of Judge Judy, has allowed me to be well acquainted with the judicial system. In my pseudo paralegal career, I am familiar with various types of evidence. Character evidence, circumstantial evidence, and forensic evidence all serve as aids when law enforcement is solving a crime. However, when it comes to the final decision of the jury, the type of evidence that is most powerful is direct evidence.

The Bible provides a narrative in which King Saul requested direct evidence of vengeance performed on his behalf. His demand—strange as it may seem—is for David to collect one hundred enemy foreskins (1 Sam. 18:25). The demand for David to collect one hundred "penis parts" was to ensure proof that the men were actually dead. This bizarre request makes more sense when we understand the importance of who these men were and why Saul wanted them killed.

Circumcision was a requirement of the Mosaic Law for all males in the family of God. The one hundred targeted men were Philistine men, who stood outside of God's covenant. They were enemies of God's people because they were violent. King Saul must have taken notes from Laban, who used manipulation when it came to identifying a husband for his daughter (see Astounding Truth #95). His daughter Michal was in love with David. The assignment to kill one hundred Philistine men was a trap. King Saul assumed that David would be killed going into this battle. However, he was proved wrong because God gave David success beyond measure. David actually killed two hundred enemy soldiers and was given Michal as his wife, entering the royal family (1 Sam. 18:27).

The success that God allowed for David in the battle against the Philistine army was a turning point in the relationship between Saul and his son-in-law, David. They became enemies, and as a result, Saul set himself up against God. Throughout this story, we are given glimpses of God's faithfulness toward David because he continually gave God the credit for his military successes. When Philistine warlords came to attack David and his army, David was prepared for battle. This made David grow in popularity. God's choice for David as King of Israel correlated well with David's choice for God. Unfortunately, the opposite is true for dear ol' father-in-law in this story. This story also serves as a reminder that sometimes godly people like David will suffer through no fault of their own.

Lord, grant me the perseverance to remain steadfast in my commitment toward You when ungodly people like King Saul involve themselves in evil schemes. Allow me success in advancing Your kingdom in the platform You have provided me, just as you did for King David. Help me to boldly give credit to You for my successes. Bless me with Your peace in living the calling You have placed over my life. Amen.

The Bloody Truth of Great Faith

Now a certain woman had a flow of blood for twelve years, and had suffered many things from many physicians. She had spent all that she had and was no better, but rather grew worse. When she heard about Jesus, she came behind Him in the crowd and touched His garment. For she said, "If only I may touch His clothes, I shall be made well."
—MARK 5:25–28

Whatever I do, I always give 100%. This is a standard I have set for myself. Of course, that does not apply to my regular standing appointments at the American Red Cross to donate blood, in which case I only give one pint. As a proud owner of the Red Cross eight-gallon pin, suffering numerous cuts that required sutures, and identifying as a female who has a regular twenty-eight-day cycle, I can confidently say I know something about bleeding. So does the unnamed woman in Mark 5:25. This woman bled consistently for twelve long years. Mark notes that she spent all she had on physicians, only to discover her problem grew worse over time.

Obvious to the female reader, this poor woman would have been physically weak from the constant blood loss. Besides physical suffering, this woman would have suffered emotionally because she was considered ceremonially unclean and unable to worship with others in the temple (see Leviticus 15, and praise God for the New Covenant!). Her desperation for healing was glaringly obvious. When she received news that Jesus was in town, she approached Him from behind and touched his clothes. Her faith triggered her miraculous and immediate healing. Jesus said, "Daughter, your faith has made you well. Go in peace and be healed of your affliction" (Mark 5:34).

Jesus did the exact opposite of what other religious leaders would have done at the time. A card-carrying, law-abiding Pharisee may have stigmatized her for the circumstance of being unclean. Yet, Jesus modeled a refreshing and new way of showing the love of God to His followers. He responded with peace, acceptance, and grace, as well as lovingly calling her "daughter." Ultimately, she received her healing because of her bold faith in seeking Jesus. By reaching out and grabbing His robe, she put her trust in His hands. These red-letter words of Jesus cause us to come to terms with our own struggle with faith.

Our wounds, grief, burdens, and daily stressors all require a certain level of healing. Jesus is the One we should turn to, believing in faith that He will redirect the circumstances as He sees fit. Jesus sees our struggles. He also sees our faith, and is faithful to bless us in our trials. Let this testimony of the faith remind you to be steadfast in seeking the Lord during your seasons of pain.

Lord, you know my physical ailments. Meet me in my seasons of isolation and show me what it means to boldly live in faith to trust You for healing, according to Your timeline. Allow me the wisdom to respond with compassion when I see others who are outside the margins of society when my flesh wants to stigmatize them. Let me model great faith in the One who has the power to heal. Amen.

-›››››‹‹‹‹-

The Birth Announcement that Changed the World

For unto us a Child is born, Unto us a Son is given; And the government will be upon His shoulder. And His name will be called Wonderful, Counselor, Mighty God, Everlasting Father, Prince of Peace.

—ISAIAH 9:6

A birth announcement is a notice traditionally mailed to family and friends by the parents of a baby with the primary purpose of proclaiming the birth of the child. Typically it includes the given name of the baby, birthdate, size, birth location, and a photo. As an added bonus, some sentiments about the joy and pride of the new parents may be included to evoke emotion.

Personally, I opted for the digital birth announcement to share the exciting news of all four Weber births, knowing that it was the quickest way to alert the masses.

In most cases, a birth announcement must be created and sent out *after* the baby is born. However, in Abraham's Bosom (a Biblical term for the Kingdom of God) God's people received the world's most important birth announcement *before* the baby was born.

Isaiah wrote an accurate birth announcement with all the critical details seven hundred years before Jesus arrived. While the height, weight, and precise birth time were omitted from this announcement, Isaiah gave us the life changing details that all of humanity needed to know about this baby boy. He tells us that the Light is coming (Isa. 9:2). He reveals that through this promised baby, we will see increased joy where gloom had previously existed (Isa. 9:3). He wrapped up this announcement by sharing the awesome news that this baby will be called Wonderful, Counselor, Mighty God, Everlasting Father, and Prince of Peace (Isa. 9:6) How about *those* birth stats?

No other prophet provided a more accurate glimpse of the future Savior. Isaiah wrote to encourage God's people that hope was coming. In this extraordinary birth announcement, he revealed that the birth would bring forth a King. This future King would serve as a complete contrast to previous Kings who rejected God. This awaited King would be different because He would endure forever (Ps. 136:1). This King would not be a king according to the world's understanding. He would rule from a cross, not a throne. He would rule with humility, not with a lavish lifestyle. God appropriately sent this birth announcement to let His people know that joy was on the way. He would not come the way typical kings arrived, and His birth story would be completely unique.

Jesus was born to restore our broken relationship with God. He is more than just a convenient talking point during holiday festivities. He came to earth on a mission to live, die, and resurrect so *all* people could experience eternal life. He knew the problem with humanity. This problem the Bible describes is found in Isaiah 53:6 stating that, "All we like sheep have gone astray; We have turned, everyone, to his own way; And the Lord has laid on Him the iniquity of us all." His solution to the problem was perfect. Isaiah wrote these words so his people knew the truth of what was to come—that He has a plan for His people, to pile on all of their brokenness and sin on to this awaited baby boy.

Lord, thank you for the gift of Your son. Allow me the peace to believe that Your plan for salvation is the ONLY way to experience eternal life. Thank you for the awaited Messiah and for the relationship I can have with Him. Thank you for providing a plan for Your people to experience Your peace. Amen.

Stephen Gets Stoned

And they stoned Stephen as he was calling on God and saying, "Lord Jesus, receive my spirit."

—ACTS 7:59

The Bible tells us that Stephen got stoned while boldly proclaiming the message of Jesus. It was a joint effort, as both Paul and Stephen lived boldly sharing the message of Christ to Jewish believers. The Merriam-Webster dictionary definition of the adjective *stoned* is "being under the influence of a drug[4]." For clarity, the Bible does not describe St. Stephen inhaling cannabis to experience an altered state of mind. Stephen getting stoned described in Acts 7:58 is a completely contrary scenario to the modern understanding of the word. In ancient Israel, stoning was the standard form of capital punishment. This stoning that took place in year 36 occurred when heavy rocks were hurled at Stephen. This event put Stephen on the record board in Christianity's Hall of Fame as the first martyr of the faith.

After the death of Jesus, the disciples were summoned to seek out seven men of good reputation, full of the Holy Spirit, and wisdom (Acts 6:3). These men were elected by the apostles to continue the mission of preaching Christ. The Bible lists Stephen as the first in this litany of faithful servants. He was the

---

4   Merriam-Webster.com Dictionary, s.v. "stoned," accessed August 17, 2023, https://www.merriam-webster.com/dictionary/stoned.

most popular because of his spiritual gift (see 1 Cor. 12) as an evangelist, which promoted him to the spotlight when speaking to the Jewish supreme court.

Stephen's enemies could not win on the merits of his arguments, so they proposed a barbaric plan to end his life. Twisting his words completely, they presented to the religious leaders the idea that Stephen had blasphemed God and Moses. Blasphemy is speaking profanity and showing lack of reverence about God, and was punishable by death in first century Israel.

In reality, Stephen presented the truth of how the ancient rituals of the Law transitioned to the new order brought by Jesus. He gave testimony of a new way of worshiping God, made possible by the death and miraculous resurrection of Jesus. Stephen did not hold back the truth. Because of his commitment to speaking with candor, he earned a popular reputation and caused friction among the religious leaders who were loyal to the teachings of the Jewish Law. This ultimately led to his demise.

The Bible gives us another *joint* reference to display Stephen's anger before he died, with his comment on how spiritually stubborn his opponents were. This reference describes the body's pivot joint located just below the head. He calls the Jewish leaders "stiff necked" (Acts 7:51) for their headstrong disobedience to the message of the Gospel. This infuriated the religious leaders, yet Stephen remained calm, completely unphased by their anger. He looked to heaven and had a vision of Jesus. Immediately after, he was dragged out to the city and stoned to death for his unwavering belief in the Gospel message.

Lord, when I am faced with opposition for my faith in Christ, help me to be bold in my commitment to sharing the Good News of what Jesus has done for all people. Allow me to have mercy on those who wrongly respond to the Truth of Christ. Like Stephen modeled, allow me to be bold in speaking Your truth to those who struggle to believe the good news of Christ and why He came. Amen.

A Biblical Heart Transplant

Cast away from you all the transgressions which you have committed and get yourselves a new heart and a new spirit.

—*EZEKIEL 18:31*

When the prophet Ezekiel commanded God's people to find a new heart, he wasn't implying that the recent Echocardiogram completed at their last physical determined an impending coronary concern. Long before the first human to human heart transplant occurred in 1967, Ezekiel wrote about what it meant to obtain a new heart, without undergoing major surgery. Not much is known about the prophet Ezekiel, but one thing I know about him is that like Jesus, he enjoyed parables when writing to his audience. A parable is a simple story to illustrate a spiritual lesson. His words regarding getting a new heart are among his most memorable and astounding. They are also some of the most curious words of the Bible.

Ezekiel wrote to God's people in exile in 571 B.C. These people gave into disillusionment that God had abandoned them. For us today, who get the benefit of reading his words in the twenty-first century, we can relate to his message when we feel distant from God. Ezekiel used heart references to stir the feelings of his people toward God by saying, "get yourselves a new heart." He wrote this knowing that the only place you can get a proper heart transplant is *not* from the organ donor list, but from the Lord.

The concept of a spiritual heart transplant is so important to those who desire to follow Christ. A Biblical heart transplant literally means that the heart of Christ is inside you. When your doctor rests his stethoscope against your chest to hear your heartbeat, that beat should be the heart of Jesus beating. Saying yes to Christ means you discard your original heart that you are given at birth because that heart is faulty. Once a person becomes a follower of Christ, they are to live according to a new rhythm, ordained by Christ.

Any number of things can harden our hearts—control, perfectionism, trauma, resentment, disappointment, or shame to name a few. Ezekiel shares an important message in 36:26 saying, "I will give you a new heart and put a new spirit within you; I will take the heart of stone out of your flesh and give you a new heart of flesh." This means that transformation is internal. Our God is a God of rebuilding what is broken down or unusable. The transformation God's people must undergo is not only external modification. Internal revisions must occur and these changes Ezekiel speaks of are through divine intervention. Human efforts are of no consequence when heart transplants occur. By God's power, we are made new and obtain the heart of Christ in our process of sanctification. This is done by the power of the Holy Spirit, which God uses to transform anyone who is willing.

Lord, I desire for my heart of stone to be removed. Give me a heart of flesh and help me live my life in obedience to You. Give me a heart that desires to please You and continually be in Your presence. Allow me to be open to the calling of the Holy Spirit for a spiritual heart transplant. Amen.

-)))))⟩⟩⟨⟨⟨⟨⟨-

What Did the Fox Say?

On that very day some Pharisees came, saying to Him, "Get out and depart from here, for Herod wants to kill You." And Jesus said to them, "Go tell that fox, 'Behold, I cast out demons and perform cures today and tomorrow, and the third day I shall be perfected.'"

—LUKE 13:31–32

One of the most popular videos of 2013 is entitled "The Fox." It's a catchy pop song that begins with several animals listed, followed by the sound they make (dog goes woof, cat goes meow, bird goes tweet, mouse goes squeak, etc.) The litany of animals and sounds continue until the catchy refrain begins…"What does the fox say?" That curious question was sung on repeat by kids all over the world when this song went viral. However, Bible nerds like me were forced to examine the literal interpretation of that question. This is a game I frequently play, purely for entertainment purposes. I take lyrics of pop songs and reframe them with a Biblical mindset. *So. Much. Fun.*

Luke 13:32 describes the response Jesus gave when He was told that Herod wanted to kill him. To understand this, we need a short history lesson to understand why Jesus called Herod a fox. The Herod Jesus was referring to in this text was Herod Antipas (not to be confused with his dad, Herod the Great, who ruled when Jesus was born and ordered the slaughter of innocent baby boys when he received the news that Christ was born). The Herod family tree was an arborist's worst nightmare. Antipas had a history of episodes that gave him the reputation of living as an unrighteous man. The most eccentric and bizarre indication that Herod Antipas was an unfit ruler was when he prompted his stepdaughter, Salome, to dance at a banquet (Mark 6:22). Salome was promised anything she wanted, up to half the kingdom as a reward for dancing. Her request was "the head of John the Baptist on a platter" (Mark 6:25).

Jesus used the word "fox" as a metaphor to mean sly and worthless. It is clear from the text that Jesus was unmoved by the threats reported by the Pharisees. He didn't give this threat any of His time or let it occupy His headspace. He was confident that He was called by God to continue His mission until the time of His death. The mission was to reach Jerusalem, where His work would be completed. Jesus was unbothered by rumors of his death or the attempts to redirect his mission. He knew at that moment He had demons to cast out of people and healings to perform. Why waste time with ridiculous threats when He knew the outcome of God's plan for His life?

Lord, let the example of this text serve as a model of obedience when people attempt to redirect the mission that God has called me to advance His kingdom. Allow me to be unmoved by the hurdles that will come my way in my calling to serve and promote Your will. Like Jesus modeled, let me be unbothered by the threats and focus on my purpose. Amen.

The Funeral Is Better than the Party

Better to go to the house of mourning Than to go to the house of feasting, For that is the end of all men; And the living will take it to heart.

—*ECCLESIASTES 7:2*

My family has hosted four female French foreign exchange students. All of our houseguests have pointed out my exaggerated use of idiomatic expressions. This made communication confusing (and humorous) with these young women who came to the United States to improve their English skills.

My favorite idiom was birthed shortly after the US Constitution was created, when Benjamin Franklin wrote in a letter that "nothing is certain except death and taxes." This is a creative way to make the point that people are powerless to avoid the inevitable. Certain things in life cannot be bypassed, like death and taxes. Long before the United States created a document to establish fundamental laws, King Solomon wrote the book of Ecclesiastes and included some wisdom about the unavoidable death we will all face.

The book of Ecclesiastes may be perplexing to pronounce, but nevertheless, it should not be bypassed because it contains so much wisdom. It was written to God's people who knew what God expected, but were challenged by living in obedience to the Lord's precepts. The assumed author, Solomon, wrote the book as a narrated autobiography to share with readers the bizarre complexities of life. Solomon's goal in writing this book was to process how to find joy in life and remain true to the calling God had placed on His people.

Solomon opens Chapter 7 with a series of statements on death. For people who do not know God and understand the biblical worldview, the notion of death brings unrelenting sadness. For unbelievers death is *the end*, the final encore on the stage of existence. Solomon brought Truth on this important topic by writing about how the funeral is *better* than the party (Eccles.7:2) because the *heart of the wise is at the funeral and the heart of the fool is at the party.* He wrote this verse to acknowledge that you often learn more at a funeral than at a feast. The funeral provides an irrefutable perspective on the world's view of death, but a life lived in submission to God provides an understanding of the Resurrection.

Paul tells the people of Philippi that death is "far better" (Phil. 1:23) when he describes his dilemma of wanting to be with Christ, but also desiring to remain alive for the mission of advancing the kingdom of God. Paul knew wholeheartedly that the outcome of his life was in the hands of Jesus. We should desire that same understanding for our lives.

Lord, help me remember to number my days (Ps. 90:12) and that precious in the sight of the Lord is the death of his saints (Ps. 116:15). Give me a kingdom mindset regarding death and allow me to live every day for Your glory. Help me keep a kingdom view on death and use me to influence others regarding the biblical truth that the funeral is better than the feast. Amen.

Death By Big Hair

During the battle, Absalom happened to come upon some of David's men. He tried to escape on his mule, but as he rode beneath the thick branches of a great tree, his hair got caught in the tree. His mule kept going and left him dangling in the air.

—*2 SAMUEL 18:9, NLT*

O f all the things to maintain about my personal appearance, my hair typically gets the least attention. Most days a messy bun under a ball cap will serve as my preferred look. As much as I choose to ignore my mane, the Bible actually has a lot to say about hair. I found many verses that discuss the complexities of hair, including a curious story about how a young man named Absalom was killed in a hair fumble.

"Life is too short to have boring hair," was most likely the motto for Absalom, who was King David's third son. He was favored by God's people and known for his charming manners, striking features, fancy chariots, and one unique physical feature—his wild and thick hair, weighing a whopping 200 shekels (equivalent to five pounds, see 2 Sam. 14:26). We can generalize from the context clues given in the Bible that if we saw his #selfie, his hair would have been ninety percent of the photo. He may have struggled to keep his tresses under control, as well as his unrelenting desire to become the next King of Israel. Although Absalom had everything going for him on the outside, his rebellious spirit and impatience to become King ultimately lead to his strange demise.

When he thought his time had come, Absalom gathered support to take up arms against his dad for the position as king. King David was emotionally torn between his role as leader and saving the life of his son. Even before King David deployed his troops to march out into battle he commanded "for my sake, deal gently with young Absalom" (2 Sam. 18:5, NLT).

Even though King David's desire was to preserve the life of his son, Absalom's infamous hair conspired against him as he was riding along on a donkey. The hair got tangled in an oak tree, leaving him hanging from the tree to die. Even though the Bible identifies long hair as a source of strength (read about Samson who was a lifelong Nazirite in Judg. 16:17), this detail was not enough for Absalom to overthrow his father.

Absalom was attractive and known for his charm, but God knew he was not the right person for the job. The charisma of Absalom could not outshine his impatience. God showed us through the faulty character of this man that nothing worthy is instant. His inheritance—kingship—was coming, but he chose to not wait on God's timing. This curious story serves as a reminder that God's timing is always best when it comes to acknowledging His plan over our lives. When we try to get ahead of God and attempt to control plans, oftentimes we are left with an undesirable outcome that could have been avoided if submission to His authority was prioritized.

Lord, let the story of ambitious Absalom serve as a reminder that Your timing is always best. Allow me the clarity of Your will when I am in a season of waiting for my next promotion or next big assignment. Give me Your wisdom God when I have an "I can do it better," attitude and help me to repent of my pride. Amen.

Laundry Time

But who can endure the day of His coming? And who can stand when He appears? For He is like a refiner's fire And like launderers' soap.
—MALACHI 3:2

Long before Wisk introduced the world to the first liquid laundry detergent and the nagging sing-song voiceover of "Ring around the collar," the Bible had something to say about getting clothes clean. These words were brought to us by the prophet Malachi, who got the role of starring in the grand finale of the Old Testament. He got the last word in, prior to the four hundred years of silence before King Jesus was born. His critical and consistent message in his short book was simple: the awaited Messiah is coming.

The book of Malachi was written in a way that underscores the incompleteness of the Lord's work at the time of writing this prophetic book. Had God demonstrated His unfailing love for His people by bringing them out of Egypt and returning them to their homeland? *Yes*, absolutely! However, at the time of Malachi's writing, God's people were still weak, oppressed, and living in bondage to the Persians in the land God had promised to Abraham. Malachi wrote to encourage God's people that hope is near.

Malachi used a creative metaphor to illustrate how the future of God's people looks bright. A figure of *bleach*, so to speak. In full disclosure, bleach and other laundry detergents as we know them today did not exist when Malachi wrote these words. The cleaning agent used to get clothes white was made from a plant, which formed a lye type soap. Ancient launderers used this strong alkaline substance to get the ring around the collar removed and work out the hash stains on clothes. Malachi used this visual illustration "like launderers' soap" to remind people what God was telling them. The refiner's fire of judgment will burn away their disobedience, and the launderer's soap will spiritually purge God's people. This is a hopeful reminder that when Christ comes, He will cleanse the world of all impurity and every stain of sin will be washed clean.

This imagery is reemphasized in the New Testament describing the transfiguration of Jesus. Mark 9:3 states, "He was transfigured before them. His clothes became shining, exceedingly white, like snow, such as no launderer on earth could whiten them." And, if that isn't enough evidence that God values the role of cleanliness, Jeremiah wrote "no amount of soap or lye can make you clean, I still see the stain of your guilt" (Jer. 2:22, NLT). God is essentially saying sin is only effectively washed away when repentance is offered with sincerity.

Lord, help me remember that much like laundry soap, the blood of Jesus cleanses us from all our sin. Thank you for sending your Son to die for my sins. Allow me to be purified through my right relationship with you, Jesus, and be a testimony to others who do not know You. Amen.

The Original Talking Donkey

And when the donkey saw the Angel of the Lord, she lay down under Balaam; so Balaam's anger was aroused, and he struck the donkey with his staff. Then the Lord opened the mouth of the donkey, and she said to Balaam, "What have I done to you, that you have struck me these three times?"

—NUMBERS 22:27–28

In 2001 the movie *Shrek* was released, and the world was introduced to a talking donkey played by Eddie Murphy. This whimsical donkey created by DreamWorks enjoys idle chatter, makes friends easily, radiates kindness, and freaks out in the face of danger. Hollywood may have been ambitious to establish this humorous and unique character; however, the concept of the talking donkey was not birthed in the entertainment industry. The original talking donkey was found in the Bible.

This event was documented by Moses in Numbers 22. The book of Numbers is appropriately named because God instructed Moses to count (or number) all the males who were able to go to war post exodus from Egypt. The overarching theme of this book is that God's plan prevails, even when His people do not. The story of the talking donkey takes place during the time the King of Moab strongly disliked God's people because he feared they would overtake his land. Anticipating this, the king offered a healthy monetary reward to Balaam, a false prophet who worked for money. Balaam put a spell on God's people while they traveled throughout the King's land. His wishes were granted, and Balaam "cursed" the loyal and God-honoring people of Israel.

God intervened and redirected this scheming plan in a miraculous way by allowing Balaam to *bless the faithful followers of God,* instead of punishing them. When the king learned of Balaam's disobedience and refusal to curse God's people, he sent money to entice Balaam to reconsider. Though God already spoke to Balaam, the king asked again. That was a big mistake; Balaam was now confined in what he could do. As they traveled, Balaam's donkey saw an angel with a sword. The donkey frantically tried to avoid the angel, and as a result of his strange behavior, the owner started beating the donkey. Numbers 22:28 describes one of the most ridiculed texts in the Bible because of the absurdity of an animal speaking. The donkey dumbfoundedly asks, "what have I done to you, and that you have struck me these three times?"

This text provides testimony that God is sovereign, even in the most bizarre circumstances of our lives. Balaam's eyes were now open and enlightened for disobeying God's instructions. The irony is that the donkey was able to see the path better than the false prophet and tell him about it. 2 Peter 2:16 revisits this Old Testament text, reminding us that "a dumb donkey speaking with a man's voice restrained the madness of the prophet." Peter wrote these words when describing false teachers. He compared false teachers to beasts born in the wild and like predators on the prowl. Peter made this Old Testament reference in his writing so his Jewish audience could be reminded of the absurdity of false teachers. The same message applies to false teachers of today, who are often gifted in presenting a gospel that misses the mark.

Lord, thank you for this amusing story in Scripture. Thank you for changing course and not allowing Balaam to speak evil against Your people. Help me be more like Your donkey, who sees the message clearly and obeys your commands. Bless me with understanding when I am presented with a message that is in opposition to Your gospel. Open my eyes to understand Your ways through the power of Your Holy Spirit. Amen.

When Iron Floats

When they arrived at the Jordan, they began cutting down trees. But as one of them was cutting a tree, his ax head fell into the river. "Oh, sir!" he cried. "It was a borrowed ax!" "Where did it fall?" the man of God asked. When he showed him the place, Elisha cut a stick and threw it into the water at that spot. Then the ax head floated to the surface.
—2 KINGS 6:4–6, NLT

Just like twins conceived from one egg and one sperm that miraculously split and become two identical babies, the book of Kings was originally one book in the Bible. During the reign of King Azariah, the book of Kings was divided into two books. These books record the history of God's people beginning with the monarchy and are told as straightforward stories. These books also detail the facts of how God's people failed to live up to the requirements of the covenant. The unknown author (possibly Jeremiah) does not pussyfoot around with presenting the facts of what occurred during this time in the history of God's people.

It is in these books we learn about an important mentor/mentee relationship. Through Scripture we are able to understand the high value God places on followers of Christ guiding and discipling those young in the faith. Elijah was called by God to mentor Elisha. 2 Kings 2:1 describes Elijah ascending to heaven in a whirlwind. He was favored by God and as a result, God spared him from death (see Astounding Truth #74 about another Biblical rock star who avoided death). As a result of Elijah's relocation to heaven to be with the Lord, Elisha was promoted to be his successor and lead God's people.

Elisha and his friends were called to serve a mission shortly after the death of his mentor. They were chopping wood to prepare to build a house. However, as they were diligently working to accomplish this task, an ax broke and flew into the nearby Jordan River. Saddened because the ax had been borrowed, the devastated man pointed out where it dropped into the river, and Elisha whipped out a stick. Much to everyone's surprise, the ax eerily floated to the surface of the water. Elisha commanded, "pick it up for yourself" (2 Kings 6:7).

This is a story of God's provision for His people. An important detail to consider in understanding this bizarre testimony is *why* the construction was taking place. The reason this house was being built was because the current facility for housing was not large enough to accommodate all those who wanted to be trained in ministry, so Elisha was approached to give approval for the construction of a new facility. God wanted to grow the ministry opportunity, so he allowed the expansion. The loss of this tool was significant because iron was expensive and rare. The laborers were devastated at this loss. This unique miracle was a result of the faith displayed by Elisha to honor God and show His people that because of their faith, God did not put a stop to His ministry expansion. This story serves as a reminder for us today that when God wants to promote ministry to expand His Kingdom, He will allow it to happen, regardless of the challenges that are thrown our way.

Lord, as strange as it would have been to witness a piece of iron float to the surface of the water, I acknowledge that this is a testimony of how You work to support the efforts of mission work. Thank you for Your word, which allows me to better understand how You work for the good of those who love You to redirect situations for Your glory. Amen.

-》》》》《《《《-

The Buzz On Wisdom and Foolishness

Dead flies putrefy the perfumer's ointment and cause it to give off a
foul odor; So does a little folly to one respected for wisdom and honor.
—ECCLESIASTES 10:1

I have already disclosed my love of idioms in Astounding Truth #66, but Ecclesiastes 10:1 proves that God loves idioms as much as I do. A fly in the ointment is an idiomatic expression used to refer to a single thing or person that ruins an enjoyable experience. My kids put me in that category when I say no to bottomless junk food opportunities. I put my kids in that category when sibling contentions disrupt the peace of my home and trigger my sin. Ah, the process of sanctification is such a gift! Thank you Lord, your mercies are new every day, and I need them every day as a parent.

Wise King Solomon coined this phrase about dead flies and used it in a litany of proverbial statements about life, specifically to help us understand the contrast between wisdom and foolishness. King Solomon was the perfect person to write about this juxtaposition. He exhibited foolish tendencies which include marrying pagan women, marrying too many women (seven hundred!), and mixing elements of pagan worship with actual worship of the Lord (1 Kings 11). However, King Solomon modeled many wise traits we can aspire to model. Solomon's love for God was exemplary, he asked God for wisdom, he built a temple for God, and his doctrine of prayer was spot on.

Solomon is essentially saying in Ecclesiastes 10:1 that a little bit of foolishness will destroy much wisdom. Stated in plain English, fools make their stupidity known. They do not expect to hide it. Any foolishness will completely cancel any wisdom. Any little bit of foolishness will contaminate a great reputation and stink it up, so to speak. Solomon loved to write about wisdom and foolishness because his life choices allowed him to experience the outcome of each. Following his bug analogy he moved to contrasting people who are directionally challenged (the fool). He used creative language to reinforce the concept that whichever way a wise person goes, you can guarantee that the fool will head the other way. He writes, "A wise man's heart is at his right hand, but a fool's heart at his left" (Ecclesiastes 10:2).

Today our challenge is to prayerfully discern how to avoid folly and seek wisdom from the Lord. In the New Testament, James provides a plan for this. He tells us to simply *ask* God for wisdom (for more on wisdom, please see Astounding Truths #75 and #93).

Lord, by Your grace, help me not to be foolish. Choosing the path of wisdom is Your desire for me. Allow me clarity of mind when faced with making this decision. Forgive me for my choices during the seasons of my life where acting in folly was comfortable for me. Remind me to submit to Your authority and ask you for clarity on how to be wise. Amen.

God Hates Sin

Then immediately an angel of the Lord struck him, because he did not give glory to God. And he was eaten by worms and died.

—ACTS 12:23

D*iary of a Worm* is a children's book written in the first-person narrative that chronicles the highs and lows of life as a worm. I have read this humorous story many times to my son, Luke, and love it for the witty diary entries that enlighten the reader on all things related to life as an annelid. However, this book was not the first to describe a diary entry from the life of a worm. Dr. Luke, author of the Book of Acts, records the history of the early church and wrote about worms in the first century to provide a biblical object lesson to teach us about how the Lord despises sin.

Shortly after Jesus died, King Herod Agrippa I ruled Judea. His name should have had a few letters swapped out to be reconfigured to *King Horrid*. This man came from a long line of savage men who were horrible on all levels (see Astounding Truth #65). His family tree looked like an anxiety attack for an arborist. Gospel writer Luke describes the scene in the book of Acts by telling us that one day when Herod was dressed in his royal apparel he gave a speech. The people responded with excitement saying, "this is the voice of god, not of man." Herod should have given praise to the Lord, but instead, allowed himself to be called a god. Immediately an angel of the Lord struck him because he did not give glory to God. He was struck down, eaten by worms, and died (Acts 12:23).

If Doreen Cronin included this feast in her children's book, it would have been recorded like this: Dear Diary: Today my pals and I devoured savage King Herod. It was a delicious and filling meal, made possible by the king's arrogance and unwillingness to give credit to God. However, the aftermath was ideal. Because of Herod's choice, the ministry of God's Word grew by leaps and bounds (Acts 12:24).

Shocking? Probably not, given the demonstrative and insufferable lineage that Herod comes from. Looking at his family tree, you can see both the roots and branches have quite a bit of damage. His grandpa was King Herod the Great, or not-so-great, because he was unstable and an insecure leader serving at the time Jesus was born (Matt. 2:3). Not only did grandpa have a few personality quirks, he killed his best loved wife *and* two of his own sons. However, the most shocking thing he did was attempt to overthrow the Lord's preordained plan and rebel against God when he received news of the arrival of Jesus. This "great" king was so unsettled over the news of the birth of the actual Great King Jesus, that he ordered all boys in the region under age two to be killed. It is clear that the apple didn't fall far from the tree in this family. However, God used these curious circumstances to magnify his power and authority. He is sovereign in all the details, even over the bizarre circumstances of the Herod family.

Lord, help me remember that when I am praised for my skills and success, that all the glory goes to You. Let me boast only in the work that You have done in my life, not on my merits. Let this text serve as a reminder of how much You hate sin. Allow me Your understanding that You are sovereign in Your plans. Amen.

-꙰꙰꙰꙰꙰꙰-

Knot Again

That we may buy the poor for silver, And the needy for a pair or sandals—Even sell the bad wheat?"

—AMOS 8:6

K not again! Did God really use a shoe reference to teach His people about taking advantage of poor people? In the case of Cinderella, one shoe really did change her life. In the case of Dorothy, her ruby red slippers were the most memorable part of her iconic look. However, in the case of Amos, God chose to rely solely on a shoe analogy to teach His people about exploiting the poor. God cares for the impoverished, and His word confirms that He has not forgotten those who are poverty stricken. Psalm 41:1 says, "Oh, the joys of those who are kind to the poor."

Little is known about the minor prophet Amos. Scripture tells us he was a shepherd and cared for sycamore fig trees before God called him to prophesy to His people (Amos 7:14). Like shoes, which are sold in pairs, Amos presented a pair of sin issues throughout his book: idolatry and social injustice. He writes about the wealthy people in God's family who chose to live unjustly and treat the disadvantaged without concern. This mindset was completely counter cultural to how the people of Israel *should* have responded to those in poverty. The Bible gives clear instructions on how followers of Christ should "speak up for the poor and helpless, and see that they get justice" (Prov. 31:9, NLT).

Having worked in the crop business, Amos used produce references. Chapter 8 is entitled "A Vision of Summer Fruit." Amos describes God showing him a basket of ripe fruit and telling Amos that He is about to call it quits with the people of Israel. God reveals He is no longer pretending everything is just fine with His people taking advantage of the weak. God expresses through Amos his explicit concern that the rights of the poor be protected while they are sold into slavery, even for insignificant debts as illustrated by a pair of shoes. God's view on slavery is carefully limited by the law of Moses, and God does not want His people exploited. Abusing the poor was never overlooked by God. His care and concern for all people—regardless of economic status—is not forgotten.

This message is repeated by Jesus in the New Testament when he says in Luke 6:20 "Blessed are you who are poor, For yours is the kingdom of God." This promise means that the poor will inherit something far greater than any of the world's riches. Jesus continues to say that those who suffer now will not suffer in the kingdom of heaven. Let these red letter words of Christ serve as a prominent reminder that His promise of the Kingdom that is to come far outweighs the struggles we face on this side of the cross.

Lord, allow the words of Amos to serve as a reminder that You gave us a kingdom view on how to respond to poverty. Bless me with a heart to love and care for the poor as a testimony of Your faithfulness in my life. Equip me with the skills to love and care for those on the margins of society. Help me be generous with the resources I have been given. Amen.

-》》》》《《《《-

God Honors our Walk

So all the days of Enoch were three hundred and sixty-five years. And
Enoch walked with God; and he was not, for God took him.
—GENESIS 5:23–24

I don't wear a Fitbit, but if Enoch got on board with this tech savvy tracker, he would have had hard evidence that he slayed his fitness goals. His step counter would hit maximum capacity, and his heart, we can only assume, would be exceptionally healthy. We know this because Genesis 5:24 tells us he had a preferred cardio workout. His preference was walking, and he did a lot of it. If only I could model that kind of consistency with my exercise routine.

The "walking" Enoch did was not the same as my favorite low impact form of exercise. This walking did not require any special shoes with orthotic inserts. The walking that triggered a biblical shout out was obtained by a steady and consistent relationship with the Lord. Enoch was a man of humility and modeled what a right relationship with God looks like, even while living in the midst of a crooked and perverse generation. Enoch was a pure man living in a very impure world. He was only three generations removed from the days of Noah when God wiped the earth clean to rid the world of everyone who lived with no regard for God (see Gen. 6:11).

Enoch's life was demonstrated by a daily pattern of faithfulness in seeking God's will. His walk took him to everyday and ordinary places, while he lived out everyday responsibilities. This walk was so extraordinary that Enoch bypassed the experience of physical death. God took Enoch directly from earth into His presence (Gen. 5:24). Of all the Old Testament saints, only Enoch and Elijah did not experience physical death (2 Kings 2:11).

We can learn a great deal from Enoch, this Biblical Hall of fame celebrity. We see that Enoch's walk was visible. Even though Enoch lived in a time of corruption, he tried to honor God with constant devotion and obedience. God rewarded his faithfulness by sparing him the pains of physical death because Enoch's walk was so precious to God. Enoch is mentioned in the New Testament in the book of Hebrews as one of the saints who modeled faithfulness to God, despite the chaos and sin surrounding their lives (Heb. 11:5). Let this testimony of Enoch's life be a reminder to not let the ungodly practices of our modern times encroach on our desire to live a life that honors and pleases God.

Lord, Your Word gives me encouragement for life after death. Let the testimony of Enoch and Elijah inspire me to live a life of honor and devotion to You during the years You have ordained for me to live on earth. Thank you for the reminder that walking closely with you is the foundation of a life that will lead me to the hall of fame as modeled in Hebrews 11. Help me to walk in love (Eph. 5:2) at all times. Amen.

-꒷꒦꒷꒦-

Two Postpartum Prostitutes

"Therefore give to Your servant an understanding heart to judge Your people, that I may discern between good and evil. For who is able to judge this great people of Yours?"

—1 KINGS 3:9

The Bible gives us many verses on seeking wisdom. However, my favorite wisdom verse describes when God met King Solomon in a dream. When asked by God, "What shall I give you?" (1 Kings 3:5), Solomon replied with a profound and comprehensive answer. First, Solomon acknowledged the great blessing of how kind God was to his dad, King David, by giving David a son to take over the throne. Then Solomon was completely honest with God, confessing to God that he is young and inexperienced, showing his humility before God. And finally, Solomon specifically requested for God to give him an understanding heart to discern between good and evil. This prayer request pleased the Lord (1 Kings 3:10).

The Astounding Truth to glean from this heartfelt and honest dialogue that took place in dreamland is how our dialogue with God should look. Solomon did not ask for the typical desires of other kings we read about in the Bible. He did not request a long life, fancy chariots, an opulent palace, or death to his enemies—he asked for wisdom because he understood the value of serving his people with a wise and discerning spirit.

God heard Solomon's prayer and blessed him with precisely what he asked for. Not only did God give Solomon what he requested, but he allowed Solomon an odd scenario to display his wisdom involving two postpartum prostitutes. Scripture tells us the two women were housemates and one of the women lost her son to suffocation when his mom rolled over on him while sleeping. In an obvious state of devastation, she swapped her dead son for the living infant of her roomie. There was no fooling her roommate; she knew the baby she woke up with was not the baby she had borne (1 Kings 3:21).

The snafu was reported to King Solomon. Unable to determine which woman was truthful, he delivered a shocking command: "Bring me a sword…cut the living child in half and give half to each mother." Gasp! I imagine you could hear a pin drop on the palace floor. The woman who was the rightful mother of the living baby was filled with compassion for her son and commanded the king to give the grieving mother her son. The lying mother's reply was a showstopper: "let him be neither mine nor yours, but divide him" (1 Kings 3:26). What a testimony of God's answer to Solomon's heartfelt prayer. We see wisdom displayed by Solomon in a unique (and odd) response to the circumstance. The infant was returned to the first woman, as it was clear to Solomon that she was the rightful mother.

Lord, I desire Your wisdom when faced with decisions. Bless me with wisdom like King Solomon modeled when faced with challenges that involve critical decisions, especially in caring for the young and vulnerable. Allow me Your vision to fully submit my desire for wisdom into Your hands. Amen.

Personal Reflection on the Curious and Miraculous Parts of the Bible

- What have you learned about God from reading Part III of Astounding Truths?
- How has your understanding of the Bible been challenged from reading some of the metaphors and idioms of the Bible? Does this writing style help or hurt your understanding of God's Word?
- There are twenty-one dreams recorded in the Bible; has God ever spoken to you through a dream?
- There are many miracles recorded in the Bible; have you seen God perform a miracle in your life?
- What has surprised you from Part III of Astounding Truths?

PART IV

God Equips His People

The final section of *Astounding Truths of the Bible* is about testimonies of how God has equipped His followers. The verb *equipping* can mean different things in this context. God equips us with His understanding when our flesh wants to dominate our thoughts; He equips us with strength when circumstances seem overwhelming or impossible; He equips us with skills to get tasks complete that He has ordained for our lives; He equips us with His presence in seasons of trial. The remaining Astounding Truths highlight some of my favorite verses on how God equips His people—by the power of the Holy Spirit—and provides us with tools to live a life that honors God.

As I write these words, I am three hours from receiving my license to serve as a foster mom (Lord willing, and my TB test is negative!) With certification in place, I am five hours away from welcoming a beautiful two-year-old island girl into our home. Serving as a wife to one man, a mom to five kids, and a writer to many is not something I can do on my own strength. Yet, God has given me a calling, and He will equip me according to His purposes. I love the words Paul wrote to the Thessalonians to encourage them in his first letter. He wrote, "God will make this happen, for He who calls you is faithful" (1 Thess. 5:24, NLT). Paul needed his audience to know that not only is God working in their lives, but that He is faithful to see them through the things He has called them to. Even though the experience of fostering will be challenging, emotional, and overwhelming for my large family, He will equip me according to His purposes in this journey because He has called me into this role.

May God bless your understanding of how He has equipped you for His purposes. May these testimonies encourage you as you continue to journey through these remaining Astounding Truths of the Bible. God bless you for your faithful commitment to seeking Truth.

God Equips Us to Understand Our Identity

"Once you had no identity as a people; now you are God's people.
Once you received no mercy; now you have received God's mercy."
—1 PETER 2:10, NLT

Let's not get overzealous with the message to our youth that they can *be anyone they want to be.* The police call that identity theft, and it is a class 1 felony. Today more than ever, and (no) thanks to the accessibility of the Internet, it is easy to get tripped up in misunderstanding our identity. If we are not discerning, we can allow things other than God to define our identity.

The message from the world on this topic is quite different from the Biblical message. Some say our identity is in our status or profession. Others may say our identity is in our popularity, political affiliations, or perhaps an identity in our religious denomination. Our identity can be misshaped based on the influences of our family, the education system, or teachers of false gospels. Misinformation is common when it comes to understanding our identity. The mission of *Astounding Truths of the Bible* was birthed from a desire to enlighten people with Biblical Truth of who they are in Christ.

It is *astounding* when we examine the biblical understanding of identity. Scripture is explicitly clear on communicating my identity—my identity is a royal daughter of God. Once I began thinking accurately about myself in those terms, it changed my outlook on who I am.

Joshua felt the same way during his season of leading God's people after the death of Moses. God equipped Joshua with words of wisdom for how to have success wherever he went:

> Be strong and of good courage, for to this people you shall divide as an inheritance that land which I swore to their fathers to give them. Only be strong and very courageous, that you may observe to do according to all the law which Moses my servant commanded you; do not turn from it to the right hand or to the left, that you may prosper wherever you go.
>
> —JOSHUA 1:6–7

God did not suggest that Joshua be strong and courageous; he *commanded* it. Through these verses, God tells us to meditate on Scripture and carefully observe everything written in it. Much like our identity, the path for success looks different for followers of Christ. Success for Christians is fulfilling the God given purpose He has ordained for our lives.

As a daughter (or son) of God, once you are a follower of Christ, this is now your heritage. Paul reminded the Galatians this profound truth: "For you are all sons of God through faith in Christ Jesus. For as many of you as were baptized into Christ have put on Christ. There is neither Jew nor Greek, there is neither slave nor free, there is neither male nor female; for you are all one in Christ Jesus" (Galatians 3:26–28). Nothing that divides us as far as worldly classifications (ethnicity, economic status, career path, political affiliation, etc.) speaks to our identity—only the Lord Jesus can speak to our identity. He equips us to understand this truth through His Word.

Lord, if I ever find myself in an identity crisis, let me rely on You for clarity. Equip me to be aware that You define my identity, not the world. Remind me on a daily basis to see myself as You see me. You alone get to say who I am. Silence the voice of the world, my peers, and the Internet when those voices speak loudly and try to replace who You say I am. Amen.

-»»»»«««-

God Equips Us for a Heart Exam

The human heart is the most deceitful of all things, and desperately wicked. Who really knows how bad it is? But I the Lord, search all hearts and examine secret motives. I give all people their due rewards, according to what their actions deserve.

—JEREMIAH 17:9–10, NLT

During the writing season of my life, I made the transition from extreme extrovert to homebody-introvert. When I said yes to this project, that meant I traded my socialite lifestyle for a quiet life alone. Most days my fingers dance atop an HP laptop supported by a painted desk I refinished in the corner of my bedroom. A struggling Monstera plant sits beside me, desperate for some attention. R.C. Sproul's *Study Bible* fights for space next to Tony Evans' *Commentary Bible*. These two men compete for my attention, along with Tara-Leigh Cobble, who brings a refreshing and feminine perspective to my workspace.

The quiet and lonely life is a new season for me. However, if you want to see me get rowdy, walk me through the journal or décor section of any big box store and examine the messages with me. Phrases like "follow your heart" and "do what makes you happy" and "just be YOU" plaster the aisles and are found on oversized wall canvases that are intended to outfit my home or my teenage daughter's bedroom. So pretty. Also, so unbiblical.

No need to take my word on this. Read the words of the prophet Jeremiah, who boldly stated that the heart is deceitful above all things and desperately wicked. Modern Bible translations use the phrases like "beyond cure" and "desperately sick" when describing our heart. It's like our heart has an incurable sickness. Jeremiah is describing the nation of Judah's sin condition in this text. This nation serves as a metaphor for the human condition. Theologians refer to this as total depravity; I refer to it as my fleshly tendencies (see Astounding Truth #29).

Jeremiah compares the heart to a puzzle that no one can figure out. However, our heart is more than a little organ that is filled with a vast sea of emotions. God actually created our heart for more than holding feelings. Our heart serves as a tool to test and examine our mind. Jeremiah wrote these words to remind us that we are able to deceive ourselves very easily. We don't know ourselves as well as we think we do.

The message of the gospel is countercultural today, and phrases that encourage a mindset of ourselves being the center of the universe or the hero in our own story are not true. If you are a follower of Christ, you do not need to depend on your efforts to get by—we've got Jesus for that.

Our identity is secure in Him (revisit the previous Astounding Truth if you need a reminder about identity). The problem I have with the notebook cover that boldly states "just be you" in gold foil is that "me" apart from Christ is actually pretty nasty. I'm prideful, short tempered, grouchy, and self-righteous. I don't want to be me anymore—I want to be transformed into the person God has created me to be, through His amazing grace.

Lord, allow me Your discernment when worldly messages creep into my environment. The flesh speaks loudly, but You, God have the power to turn my attention to thoughts of You and Your Word. Help me remember that Your mission for me is not happiness, but holiness through my sanctification process. Thank you for reminding me how deceitful my heart can be. Amen.

God Equips Us to Wash Some Feet

If I then, your Lord and teacher, have washed your feet, you also ought to wash one another's feet. For I have given you an example, that you should do as I have done to you.

—JOHN 13:14–15

Years ago, I read a popular book with my book club about washing your face. This book was a collection of motivational tips, Bible quotations, and author testimony of lessons learned for reclaiming your life and achieving happiness. I certainly commend the author for her boldness to share her words with the world.

Writing is not what you start or what you finish. It is about what you start, finish, and put out for the world to see. While this book achieved unprecedented success (#2 book on Amazon in 2018), I was ankle deep in disappointment in the lack of clarity regarding the Gospel message. A book published from a Christian perspective involving the topic of washing body parts should be about washing feet, not the face.

John 13 describes the dirty little secret modeled by Jesus to his disciples. Jesus washed the feet of his closest friends the night before He died as an object lesson to model what their life was going to look like after He was gone. This was done before the Passover meal, which we refer to today as *The Last Supper*. If you are a church goer, you may have seen this celebrated during Holy week (the week leading up to the celebration of the Lord's Resurrection, commonly known as the pagan word *Easter*). Some Christians celebrate foot washing and call it *Holy Thursday*, some use the phrase *Maundy Thursday*, and some call it the *Upper Room Celebration* (taken from the text that identifies that Jesus washed the feet of his friends in an upstairs room).

Practically speaking, foot washing was a common element of hospitality before a meal in the first century. People wore sandals as they commuted by foot on dusty roads. Servants performed this chore as a way to show honor to guests, which explains why Peter emphatically refused the cleaning services of Jesus (John 13:8). Jesus did not like Peter's response. He replied, "If I do not wash you, you have no part with Me."

Jesus said this knowing the details of what His next 24 hours would look like. He knew He was about to be betrayed by Judas, one of his closest friends. He knew He would be beaten, made fun of, and nailed to a cross as an innocent man among criminals. Yet, he wanted to equip His followers with one final lesson on the importance of serving others. The choice made by Jesus for selecting a practical, necessary, and menial task to perform serves as a reminder that we are also to serve others.

The kingdom mindset declares that we are not born for our personal benefit, but to *serve the people God has placed in our lives*. Gulp. I feel this statement with the intensity of a toddler's tantrum when the demands for Cocomelon are not honored quick enough. *I am to serve my family not only because God has allowed me the great pleasure of being a wife and mom, but also to model what He did for His followers.*

What Jesus modeled in this text is completely backward to what is commonplace in our society. We are instructed to care for others and show the same kind of love Jesus did to his followers. John 13:15 records some memorable words spoken by Jesus. He said, "I have given you an example, that you should do as I've done for you." This verse reminds us to love and serve people when it is uncomfortable or requires personal sacrifice. It reminds us to love and serve people even when fleshly desires prefer our attention. It reminds us that we are never too important or too powerful to set our preferences aside for the needs of others.

Lord, give me a Kingdom mindset when it comes to washing the feet of others. Allow me to serve others with joy for Your glory and provide opportunities for me to show love to others by washing the feet of the people You have placed in my life. Whether it is the tiny feet of my kids, or the big feet of our coworkers, equip us to carry out the mission of the gospel to the world. Amen.

-»»»«««-

God Equips Us To Honor Him In An Ungodly Culture

But Daniel purposed in his heart that he would not defile himself with the portion of the king's delicacies, nor with the wine which he drank; therefore he requested of the chief of the eunuchs that he might not defile himself.

—*DANIEL 1:8*

G od shows us in the Bible that even holy heroes have a shadow side. Moses committed murder (Exod. 2:12); David committed adultery (2 Sam. 11:4); Noah got drunk and naked (Gen. 9:21); Solomon was a sex addict (1 Kings 11:1); Sarai was scheming (Gen. 16:3); Jacob was a deceiver (Gen. 25:31); Daniel was … um.… hmm… If you struggle to find any dirt on Daniel, I suggest that you put that search to bed. The Bible offers no dirt on Daniel. He is as clean as the new fallen snow (Ps. 51:7).

Daniel was a faithful man of God and although he lived 2,500 years ago, his testimony has a modern vibe. The lesson we learn from Daniel's model of faithfulness is completely relevant in the twenty-first century. As a teenager, Daniel was taken from his homeland of Jerusalem to pagan Babylon (near modern day Baghdad, Iraq) where he experienced massive culture shock. A man named King Nebuchadnezzar had conquered the land of God's people. In an attempt to strengthen his kingdom of Babylon and weaken the conquered land of God's people, King Nebuchadnezzar took the smartest and best-looking young men for military training (Dan.1:4).

Daniel became a red flag not only for his unblemished physique, but also because his commitment to honoring God in an ungodly culture was unwavering. Daniel and his friends serve as poster boys for anyone facing hostility for their beliefs. He refused to conform to the popular pagan teachings which were thriving where he was relocated. It was a prophetic message from Isaiah that some of God's people will be taken and made to serve in the king's palace (see Isa. 39:6–7), but Daniel would not fall prey to the world. He knew he was set apart by God and desired to maintain his loyalty to God, even in dire circumstances.

We have much to digest from the entire book of Daniel, but the primary theme of Daniel is how God's sovereignty directs the circumstances of all nations. According to His dominion, God will intervene among nations according to His plan. Daniel 4:35 gives encouragement for people in persecution, reminding us to trust God, for His plans cannot be obstructed. Daniel also encourages readers to look beyond their current circumstances toward the return of Christ, whose "dominion is an everlasting dominion" (Dan. 7:14).

The book of Daniel also serves as a tool for all those who seek to understand how God used other nations to bring discipline to His people. This was done by prophecy, prayer, and apocalyptic visions. Through this book, we learn how God equips people for spiritual warfare (see Astounding Truth #45 on how God desires we dress for battle). Daniel's life is testimony that even when circumstances are not in our favor, God is completely sovereign in His plan.

Lord, if You enabled Daniel to live a godly life in an ungodly culture, You can do the same for me. Allow me to be completely focused on pleasing and obeying You, just as Daniel did in a culture that did not honor God. Thank you for the book of Daniel that provides lessons I can learn from the life of this young man and the dangers of my pride. Amen.

-›››››‹‹‹‹‹-

God Equips Us With Weapons for War

*We are human, but we don't wage war as humans do. We use God's
mighty weapons, not worldly weapons, to knock down the strongholds
of human reasoning and to destroy false arguments.*
                                        —*2 CORINTHIANS 10:3–4, NLT*

When my husband, Bryan, received an invitation to travel on the military's
dime to the war zone of Afghanistan for a twelve-month camping
experience, we made a few trips to our favorite Recreational Equipment store
(REI) to prepare for the excursion. While the Bible does not say to visit your
favorite camping store to prepare for war, it does provide specific insights about
how to best prepare for the war that all followers of Christ will face. However, the
warfare discussed in 2 Corinthians 10 is quite different from the war the United
States faces when it comes to ridding the world of terrorists.

Paul—the GOAT evangelist—wrote an insightful and relevant message to
the people of Corinth about spiritual warfare. Spiritual warfare is the inward
and outward battle we face against the enemies of God (mainly Satan and his
minions). It was once a topic I skirted around, not confident enough to address
reality when I felt the spiritual attacks. These attacks came in seasons when my
desire and commitment to do Kingdom work was the most intense.

Paul wrote on spiritual warfare to this city in modern day Greece because
it had a reputation for debauchery. People were drawn to Corinth because of its
reputation for loose living. Paul was confident that he was called by God to travel

to Corinth to aid in redirecting the sinful behavior the Corinthians were thriving at. He desired to deal with the sin and shortcomings of the Corinthian people directly to effect change and bring them into the light of the Gospel message.

The primary challenge Paul experienced in his missionary work was tearing down the lies about him and his message. When this topic came up, Paul addressed it head on and with determination, defended his calling as an apostle, and the work he was faithfully committed to doing. Paul used military imagery when he wrote, saying that he would not fight back with real weapons. No Glock or Remington needed; he announced that he would fight spiritual warfare with prayer, Truth, and obedience. Paul was serious with his message. He knew with certainty that his opposers in Corinth were servants of Satan. Paul knew that the power of the Holy Spirit was alive and much greater than any doubts he experienced.

Paul was the perfect person to write this message, as he experienced massive hardships in his life. As a result of experiencing life in a fallen world, he also experienced feelings of defeat, fear, uncertainty, and doubt. He preached with transparency on this experience, asking his listeners to bring every thought into captivity to the obedience of Christ (2 Cor. 10:5). Sin, discouragement, and darkness always starts with a single thought, but victory or defeat depends on how you handle that thought. Through the power of God's Spirit, He will provide a way to break down the lies of the enemy and reveal Truth to everyone who is a follower of Christ.

Lord, help me to stand my ground with Truth and peace when thoughts of unrest fill my head. I ask that You tear down the strongholds of the Enemy in my mind and equip me with the proper battle gear to fight back. Like Paul, equip me with insights on how to fight the lies of Satan. I ask the Holy Spirit to guide my thoughts to thoughts of Christ and His redemptive work on the cross. Amen.

->>>>><<<<<-

God Equips Us To Revisit Beauty Standards

The Lord says, "Beautiful Zion is haughty: craning her elegant neck, flirting with her eyes, walking with dainty steps, tinkling her ankle bracelets. So the Lord will send scabs on her head; the Lord will make beautiful Zion bald."

—ISAIAH 3:16–17, NLT

I have two sisters who work in healthcare for King Jesus. Their mission to serve with integrity in the community where God has called them keeps these women focused on the goal of serving others. When local labor unions determine that health care employees must strike, they come to work to do the job God has given them. Like the promise of scabs that God will send to punish His people, I have seen some scabs in my family and rejoice in their commitment to the mission of serving their community.

My career in Human Resources precedes my current career as a trophy wife. Although I value workers' rights, I shudder with concern for what modern labor unions have done to promote the kingdom attitude regarding work (see Col. 3:23). The drawbacks of modern unions affect organizational culture and can create unnecessary bureaucracies. Nevertheless, when the prophet Isaiah wrote about scabs, he was not referring to those who rebelled and crossed the picket line during a strike.

The entire book of Isaiah deals with a variety of issues that come with living a life that honors God. Chapter 3 begins with a description of the corrupt men called to lead. However, it is not only the men who get rebuked. Isaiah was quick to call out the wives who must also take their share of blame for the condition of the nation of Israel. The women were guilty of using their beauty to draw attention to themselves, rather than God. The imagery is not pretty (pun intended) and Isaiah used gross imagery like scabs on the scalp and rotten smells to paint a visual of how God will punish these women for flaunting their wealth and physical features (Isa. 3:17). As spouses of those in leadership, these women could have used the opportunity to influence others for Kingdom building. The sin they were guilty of was using their beauty, wealth, and position to bring glory to themselves, and not to God who provided everything (jewelry, clothing, perfume, purses, etc.; see Isa. 3:18–23) for them. Isaiah wrote a message that was clear: let your style be about God, not self.

God's message to His people is far from the worldly message about beauty. A great figure and physical beauty are things our culture pursues with vigor. Yet God, through his Word, reveals that the desire to obtain the perfect body and face can be idolatrous. Peter writes about the importance of seeking inner beauty, which is completely contradictory to what our culture says about beauty being only skin deep. "Do not let your adornment be merely outward—arranging the hair, wearing gold, or putting on fine apparel—rather let it be the hidden person of the heart, with the incorruptible beauty of a gentle and quiet spirit, which is very precious in the sight of God" (1 Pet. 3:3–4). Peter's words still apply to God's people today. The style we seek should be about our character, our love of others, and primarily our relationship with God.

Lord, quiet the world when I struggle to have peace about my physical appearance. Remind me that God's view on physical beauty is far from how the world sees beauty. Let me not be swayed by the vanity of the world. I ask that You equip me with an awareness that my beauty should always be about what is hidden in my heart, which is precious in Your sight. Let people be attracted to me for how I represent You, Lord. Amen.

-»»»«««-

God Equips Regular People

And as Peter knocked at the door of the gate, a girl named Rhoda came to answer.

—ACTS 12:13

"I'm not like a regular mom, I'm a cool mom," is a memorable line from the 2004 movie *Mean Girls*. We learn from Mrs. George, played by Amy Poehler, that being regular is unacceptable when it comes to motherhood. I agree. I strive to be extra in my calling as a mom. However, the Biblical view of regular people is extremely different from the message of the movie. Rhoda is a prime example of how God uses ordinary people to accomplish extraordinary things for His kingdom.

Rhoda is mentioned briefly in Scripture during a time of crisis for the early church. After the crucifixion of Jesus, many cynics thought the Jesus "problem" was solved by his death. They were wrong. Because God had called and equipped people like Peter and John, the number of Christ followers multiplied exponentially after the Resurrection of Jesus. As a result, religious leaders in Jerusalem got to work and began arresting (and killing) some of those who were bold to proclaim the work of Jesus. Rhoda was mentioned in the book of Acts as one of the people who gathered to pray when the news spread that Peter was arrested for his unwavering commitment to the message of Christ.

Was Rhoda a wealthy woman who hosted church services? No. Was she married to a church leader? Nope. Rhoda was just an ordinary servant woman who took part in the miraculous events that led to Peter getting out of prison because *she prayed with expectation*. The Astounding Truth of this text is that when regular people pray, God moves to do extraordinary things according to His plan. Peter was in prison sandwiched between two soldiers (Acts 12:6), with additional guards at the door, when miraculously an angel appeared and flooded the prison with light. The handcuffs fell from his wrists, and he was able to tie his shoes and exit the prison (Acts 12:8).

The Bible is loaded with testimonies of God calling and equipping "regular people" to do great things for His ministry. The men Jesus called into His immediate circle of influence were fishermen. A career as a fisherman in the first century indicates they were uneducated, but God still used these ordinary men for His purposes. David was a shepherd, but God still equipped Him to lead His people. Joshua was average, until God personally appointed him to be a soldier and successor to Moses. Rahab was a prostitute, but God used her in the lineage of Jesus. Ruth was a beggar, but God had bigger plans for her life. Joseph was a simple carpenter who received the high honor of serving as stepdad to Jesus. These people are all ordinary people doing ordinary work, yet God used them in His amazing story of redemptive work. God also uses the prayers of "regular people" to do extraordinary things. Let the message of Rhoda serve as a reminder that God will always equip the called to carry out His plans for humanity.

Lord, help me remember the example of Rhoda when I am challenged to think my regular status in society does not allow me to do important kingdom work. Remind me that God hears the humble prayers of all people who cry out to Him. Help me to pray in earnest and expect miraculous things to happen when I come before You in prayer. Amen.

-꧁꧂-

God Equips Us In Seasons of Bitterness

But she said to them, "Do not call me Naomi; call me Mara, for the Almighty has dealt very bitterly with me."

—*RUTH 1:20*

The word "bitter" is used to describe one of the four basic taste sensations. It conjures up feelings of pungent or rancid flavors in food and drinks. Thanks to my summer job at the Detroit Country Club when I was nineteen years old and the superlative preferences of the wealthy patrons, I learned why bitters are necessary to craft the perfect Old-Fashioned or Manhattan cocktail to balance out the overpowering sweet flavor.

Moses used the adjective "bitter" to describe the water God's people found when they arrived in the wilderness after the adventure of traveling through the parted Red Sea waters (Exod. 15:23). Associating the word *bitter* with food and drinks is entirely appropriate. However, the Bible offers us a glimpse of how being *bitter* can transition to being *blessed* in God's redemptive plan.

The Bible records that Naomi demanded a name change (Ruth 1:20). The name she was given at birth meant sweet. When her life turned to chaos and she grieved the death of her husband and both sons, her sweetness abated, and she became like the arugula kale salad I enjoy every afternoon to break my fast—very bitter. She said to her two daughters-in-law amid her suffering, "do not call me Naomi, call me Mara, for the Almighty has dealt very bitterly with me" (Ruth 1:20).

Naomi was in a foreign country, grieving the deaths of the three men in her life, and living in a culture surrounded by ungodly people. Her use of the word bitter referred to the intensity of her suffering in her mind and body. More notable is the fact that her choice of words identifies that she felt strongly that God allowed her suffering. In this season, she could only see her pain. Her self-focus blinded her to God's greater plan over her life.

However, God in his sovereignty did not leave Naomi helpless. He equipped her to see that she was misunderstanding the providence of God's timetable. In His perfect plan, her daughter-in-law, Ruth, remained faithful and loyal to her mother-in-law during her season of suffering. They returned together to Naomi's hometown of Bethlehem after the deaths of their husbands.

Ruth chapter one describes bitter Naomi, but three chapters later, in chapter four, we see a glimpse of a new woman. This new Naomi is holding the baby born to her daughter-in-law, Ruth, and her new husband Boaz (see Astounding Truth #3). This baby would be the grandfather of King David. This baby would eventually be the great-times-forty grandfather of Jesus. God was sovereign in His plan and used all of Naomi's pain for His purposes. May the testimony of her life serve as a reminder that our pain is never without purpose.

Lord, when seasons of suffering fall upon me, allow me to look beyond my present sufferings and know that all my pain has a purpose in Your kingdom. Allow me Your vision for the hard times and help me seek You through my grief. Give me strength to bear the heavy burdens of life. Allow me to feel Your love and compassion during my trials. Amen.

-》》》》《《《《-

God Equips Us to See that His Love Transcends Human Understanding

Beloved, let us love one another, for love is of God; and everyone who loves is born of God and knows God. He who does not love does not know God, for God is love.

—*1 JOHN 4:7–8*

The setting was a three-word location with thousands of letters—the Hagåtña Post Office. The mission—mail Christmas cards. The escort—my toddler son Levi. Knowing he would be elated if I gave him a chore to participate in, I announced that he could put the letters in the mailbox. He responded with joy, "Yeah, I get to put my ABCs in the box!"

In a Post Office setting, "letters" do not mean the same thing as "letters" of the alphabet. However, to a toddler, the two words sound the same. It was no surprise that he made a funny. The same misunderstanding applies to the word *love*, which can be defined and understood in a variety of ways depending on context. "I love Breyers Mint Chocolate Chip ice cream," is a statement I declare often; however, this is not the same as biblical love. Biblical love, or God's love is not understood as the world understands love. God's love transcends human understanding. The New Testament writers of God's Word tell us about the selfless, unconditional love of God towards the undeserving. This type of love is the standard for followers of Christ to live by. It is the model of love we are to show to others.

1 John 4:7 begins a long series of verses that outline how to know God through love. This section of Scripture begins with "let us love one another, for love is of God." This kind of love is understood as agape love, which is a Greek word that defines the fatherly love from God for all humans. This is not to be confused with eros love, which is passionate and romantic love or philia love, which is the love that kindred spirits share. Friendship love is defined as philia love.

The Bible documents many examples of philia love (David and Jonathan; Elijah and Elisha, Paul and Timothy; and Jesus and John) As if that is not enough flavors of love, C.S. Lewis in his 1960 book, *The Four Loves,* writes of the last love as storge love. This final love describes the love of family. Because of the vast variety of categories in various bookstores, we can read about love in the romance section, the children's book section, or the hobby section, but the only book that fully explains the agape love of God is the Bible. God included over sixty verses in His Word about His love and how we should love others. May we be encouraged to seek Him when we are challenged to love as Christ loves His people.

Lord, I come into Your presence. Make me aware of Your overwhelming love for me. By Your Holy Spirit, allow me to model Your love to others. Bless me as I seek to follow the example of Jesus in treating others with love. Thank You for Your unfailing love for me and how You model what perfect love looks like. Amen.

-》》》》《《《《-

God Equips Women with Virtue

O my son, O son of my womb, O son of my vows, do not waste your
strength on women, on those who ruin kings. It is not for kings, O
Lemuel, to guzzle wine. Rulers should not crave alcohol.
—PROVERBS 31:2–4, NLT

Proverbs 31 is a chapter of the Bible that makes me excited and terrified at the same time. The bulk of the chapter describes the model Christian woman. Reading through the chapter reminds me of all the ways I fall short in this category. However, the opening words of advice and wisdom given by a mother to her son about avoiding promiscuous women are my favorite (see Prov. 31:3 regarding my personal prayer for my sons). She follows with a list of requirements regarding the character of a king. As a mom to Luke and Levi, I love the encouragement I get from these verses on how to equip my sons for leadership, to stand up against injustice, and uphold righteousness—*this is a high calling for a mother of sons and should not be taken lightly.*

The humbling part of the chapter begins in verse 10, where the model woman is described. It is a sobering reminder of all the ways I can improve as a model of biblical womanhood. The Proverbs 31 woman is overwhelmingly perfect. At times she is intimidating (see verse 13, where she works diligently with her hands, knitting and sewing). While it is hard to live up to this ideal of a woman, we can thank this mother for her insights into what her fantasy future daughter-in-law should be like. The reality is that this woman may have not done all these things listed in a day, but perhaps she did them in her lifetime. She may have lived her season of entrepreneurship (verse 24) *after* she raised her family. She may have fed the poor (verse 20) *after* she lived a season of caring for her children. What an encouraging reminder that these tasks do not have to be completed in the same season.

Be encouraged by the fact that the woman described in Proverbs 31 is a woman of great faith and substance. She does not live with an attitude of entitlement. She models a hard-working woman who honors her husband and family by serving with grace. Her words are wise (verse 26), and she controls her tongue. "Her children rise up and call her blessed; her husband also, and he praises her: Many daughters have done well, But you excel them all" (Proverbs 31:28–29).

The chapter ends with an awesome reminder that the reward for this woman is that her husband and children praise her for her model of faithfulness. They value her and they make a big deal about her because they know how much she does for them. The overarching theme of the chapter is summed up in verse 30. As we know, beauty will fade, but the characteristics of a woman who fears the Lord will always be praised.

Lord, thank You for the beautiful picture You paint of the model wife and daughter-in-law. By your guidance, equip the women in my life to live this way with joy. Aid in the areas where they are weak and allow them to be guided by Your Holy Spirit. Amen.

-≫≫≫≫⟨⟨⟨⟨⟨-

God Equips His People to be Holy

As obedient children, not conforming yourselves to the former lusts,
as in your ignorance; but as He who called you is holy, you also be
holy in all your conduct, because it is written, "Be holy, for I am holy."
—*1 PETER 1:14–16*

I love a great pair of jeans. However, the *jeanius* who prompted the cringy
fashion trend of upper thigh holey jeans needs to rethink the concept of the
peek-a-boo windows over the femur. I cannot in good conscience support the
purchase of holey jeans because while I respect the desire to test fashion trends,
I do not think they are wholly successful in giving me the polished look I desire
for my mom uniform.

However, I'll always say yes to a whole margherita pizza. And I am wholly
committed to the advancement of the gospel and equipping people to learn the
Word. As daunting as the biblical command to live a holy life is, I am firm on
my commitment to this command because God calls His people to be holy. The
concept of holiness may make you feel uneasy. It's a word that stirs up a variety
of emotions. Understanding the history of God's command to be holy has helped
me gain insights on what it means to be holy today.

The concept of holiness was originally brought to light in the third book of
the Bible. In Leviticus, God gave instructions to his people who were preparing
to move into the land that was promised to them (see Gen. 12). The Bible gives
glimpses of the primary challenge of God's people at this time—they knew they

were identified as God's people but struggled to actually *live* as God's people. The environment had everything to do with this challenge because the land God ordained for His people was not vacant. God made a sovereign decision to plop them in the land that was occupied by the Canaanites and Amorites. They participated in satanic sex rituals, giving them chart topping success as the most immoral people in history. Living in that environment allowed for God's people to be easily brainwashed into thinking that living like that (offering child sacrifices, pagan occult practices, incest, and bestiality) was acceptable.

The command to be holy is emphasized by Moses throughout the book of Leviticus. His mission was to equip God's people to be confident in the fact that they should be significantly distinguished and esteemed above their neighbors. That same principle was reinforced by the apostle Peter. He was rock solid in his mission to remind Christ followers that they are to live holy, because God is holy. The world should see that God equips his followers to be different—set apart—and that we are to not conform to the world's way of living. He wrote to remind them that their former ways of living before they knew Christ should be forgotten. They were ignorant before putting their faith in Jesus, but now that they know Truth, they should live like it. Live holy, because Christ is holy.

Lord, allow me Your vision for how my life can be set apart from the sinful ways of the world. Equip me to live a holy and blameless life for Your glory. When I am tempted to live seeking the ways of the world, equip me with a desire to honor Your calling for my life. I thank you today for sending Your son Jesus to die for my sins. Amen.

-›››››‹‹‹‹-

God Equips His People to Respond to Tyranny

"When you do the duties of a midwife for the Hebrew women, and see them on the birthstools, if it is a son, then you shall kill him; but if it is a daughter, then she shall live." But the midwives feared God, and did not do as the king of Egypt commanded them, but saved the male children alive.

—EXODUS 1:16–17

Midwifery is like picking someone up from the airport, but you don't know what they look like or when the expected flight is scheduled to land. I have had the extreme honor of utilizing the services of some exceptional midwives for my pregnancy care. These midwives got the delight of catching my four babies and seeing them take their first breath. They also got the privilege of seeing and stitching my nether regions, and for that, midwifery is without a doubt holy work.

The Bible gives us a glimpse of how God used some outstanding midwives who were bold in their allegiance to the Lord over the sinful government they lived under. The testimony of Shiphrah and Puah shows that when the government is unjust, God-fearing people need to respond. We see this principle modeled by the Hebrew midwives under the tyrannical Pharaoh in Exodus Chapter 1.

Pharaoh lived in fear that God's people would rise up and destroy all the lofty ambitions of the Egyptians. His insecurity and racist tendencies triggered one of the most neurotic episodes recorded in Scripture. He ordered death to all male babies born into the family of God. The rationale behind this decision was that with no men to rise up to train and become soldiers, the people could not raise an army to defeat Pharaoh. This heinous act of murder was assigned to the midwives. But God, in his sovereignty, knew that these women were pro-life heroes. Because these midwives feared God, they did not obey as the king of Egypt commanded them (Exod. 1:17). God is the greatest pro-lifer and because of the choice to respect the sanctity of life, these women were praised and rewarded by God.

The Bible calls followers of Christ to obey the government. Romans Chapter 13 is titled *Submit to Government* and Paul tells us that every soul should be subject to the governing authorities (Rom. 13:1). This passage makes it clear that we are to obey the government that God has placed over us. We should pay the taxes we owe, obey the laws, and show respect to our elected officials. However, when the government imposes laws that are contradictory to the precepts of God, believers should seek wisdom in discerning how to uphold the commands of God before the government.

Modern times somewhat parallel the atrocity modeled in Exodus. Our government supports the termination of unborn babies by funding abortion centers with United States taxpayer support. This goes against the biblical principle regarding how God views the children He has created in His image. Let the civil disobedience modeled by Shiphrah and Puah be an inspiration for all who put their faith in God to stand firm in their commitment to uphold the value of life. The Lord gives life, and only He should take it away (see Job 1:21).

Lord, give me unashamed boldness to respond to sinful, unjust, and tyrannical elected officials who support the mission of Satan. Allow me the wisdom and discernment to see beyond the fleshly desires of sinful men and women who are standing for things that do not support the advancement of the Gospel. Give me boldness like You gave the midwives to respond with grace. Amen.

-»»»««««-

God Equips Grandparents

I remember your genuine faith, for you share the faith that first filled your grandmother Lois and your mother, Eunice. And I know that same faith continues strong in you.

—2 TIMOTHY 1:5, NLT

Both of my grandmas play a special role in the precious memories I have from my childhood. Memories of drinking cold coffee and watching *World News Tonight* with Peter Jennings flood my mind when I recall sleepovers at my Grandma Laethem's house in Detroit in the early 1980's. Grandma Lucido, my maternal grandma, lived beside a Dairy Queen and good behavior was occasionally rewarded with a Dilly Bar. Her backyard, which provided a spectacular play area for my cousins and I, had a raspberry bush, an awesome swing set, a statue of the Blessed Mother, and an enameled iron bathtub filled with plants.

The Bible sheds light on the influential role a grandmother can have in the lives of her grandchildren. Unlike the savage grandma described in Astounding Truth #32 who plotted to kill her grandbaby in an attempt to promote her success, Grandma Lois belongs in the Granny Hall of Fame for her strong and sincere faith in Christ and for the influence she had on her daughter Eunice and grandson Timothy. The genuine faith of Lois made her a model grandma and the topic of discussion among Paul and Timothy.

The letter of 2 Timothy is the final letter Paul wrote. It is a heartfelt letter to Timothy, his beloved son in the faith. Paul opens the letter reminding Timothy that he is thankful for him and appreciates Timothy's faithful service to the Gospel expansion. Paul acknowledges that Timothy is the man he is today because of the faith of his grandmother and mother. This serves as a reminder of how important a godly heritage is to a family. The earthly family is God's foundational and first platform for the transfer of faith.

By God's grace, I was placed into a family that modeled the importance of honoring the precepts of God. My grandparents and parents spoke of God and served as my first exposure to God and His character. With God leading the charge, I am committed to doing the same for my children and all the children God allows me to influence. This verse serves as a powerful reminder about the incredible opportunity I have been given to influence my kids (and future grandkids!) for God's kingdom.

Thankfully, my kids have a dad in their life who models what it looks like to live the disciplines of the Christian faith. However, Timothy did not have a dad who loved Jesus. We gain insights from the context clues in Acts 16:3 that Timothy's circumcision was done privately, as to not offend his father who was Greek (circumcision was performed on all male infants who were born into God's kingdom by Jewish roots as a sign that they were to be set apart from their Greek and Pagan companions). God was sovereign in who He used to build Timothy's faith, knowing that he did not have a father who modeled a life of submission to God. By the powerful testimony of his grandmother and mother, God equipped Timothy to do remarkable things for Christ by his faithful obedience.

Lord, equip the women in my life to be exceptional models of the faith for the upcoming generation. Thank you for those in my life who have modeled what it means to be a sold out Christ follower and who influence their children and grandchildren to be Jesus followers. Equip me to be bold for the sake of the gospel for the young people I have influence over. Amen.

-》》》》《《《《-

God Equips Us To Rejoice In Suffering

We can rejoice, too, when we run into problems and trials, for we know that they help us develop endurance. And endurance develops strength of character, and character strengthens our confident hope of salvation.

—ROMANS 5:3–4, NLT

I live with many people, and these people love to get clothes dirty. Thanks to the wonderful and modern convenience of a washing machine, I reap the benefits of clean laundry with minimal effort on my part. All I do is place the clothes in the drum, add detergent, and press the start button. The machine will twist, turn, and knock around the clothes and at the end of the cycle they come out cleaner, brighter, and better than before.

This process is a visual object lesson for going through difficult times, with God serving as the washing machine. He does the redemptive work we need to come out clean. I experienced this when I went through a difficult season after learning about a cleft lip diagnosis during a diagnostic ultrasound of Baby Weber #4. It became very comfortable for me to isolate myself from people and suffer in silence while I processed this news. However, that is contradictory to what the Bible instructs us to do when we journey through a difficult season. In our darkness, it is easy to isolate ourselves from others, but the root of a solid spiritual life is birthed in *relationship between God and His people* when we suffer.

The minor prophet Zephaniah's book is rooted with themes on the relationship between God and His people. Zephaniah refuses to accept the theology that regards God as distant and uninvolved in human affairs. "The Lord your God is in your midst" (Zeph. 3:17), is confirmation of the promise of God's dwelling in the depths of His people. The continuation of verse 17 says, "The Mighty One, will save; He will rejoice over you with gladness, He will quiet you with His love, He will rejoice over you with singing."

This verse points us to the astounding truth of God's character—that He will equip you to rejoice, even in difficult seasons. God is present at all times, equipping you with His peace during seasons of sorrow. It is a reminder of God's transforming work of creating a new person when He walks you through seasons of darkness. A similar message is presented by the Apostle Paul when he writes about sorrow. "We can rejoice, too, when we run into problems and trials, for we know that they help us develop endurance. And endurance develops strength of character, and character strengthens our confident hope of salvation" (Romans 5:3–4, NLT). These verses serve as an excellent reminder that God will always be with us; He will always direct our path, and we can rely on His wisdom in all seasons of life, through the dark and the light.

Paul writes these statements to encourage followers of Christ that God is working all of our afflictions for our good. It may not be obvious on this side of the cross, but trials are intended to create endurance, which will lead to character refinement, and eventually will increase our faith in the One who ordained the trial.

Lord, I ask for the awareness of Your presence through my trials. Allow me to be steadfast in my reliance on You through all of my ups and downs. Equip me to know that you are sovereign through the storms of life and with me at all times. Bless me with Your peace when I am faced with a situation that is difficult or uncomfortable. Amen.

-≫≫≫‹‹‹‹-

God Equips Us For His Purposes

*Then Moses said to the Lord, "O my Lord, I am not eloquent, neither
before nor since You have spoken to Your servant; but I am slow of
speech and slow of tongue."*

—EXODUS 4:10

If you have ever felt unequipped or unprepared to complete a task God has
given you, then the testimony of Moses is totally relatable. I felt unprepared
for marriage, yet I said "yes" when Bryan Weber asked me to partner with him
in a lifelong commitment. I felt unprepared for motherhood when I discovered
I was pregnant two months after I said "I do," yet I welcomed the challenge
with open arms. I felt unequipped to teach group fitness classes, yet I was out in
front of a group of ladies and gave it everything because I knew this is what my
community needed. I felt unequipped to welcome a two-year-old foster daughter
into our already chaotic home, yet I said "yes" because I knew God would equip
us with all that we needed to care for her during a season when she needed a
loving and safe home.

Moses felt completely unequipped for the assignment of speaking to Pharaoh.
In this conversation, Moses needed to request that Pharaoh set God's people
free to return to their land. At the time God gave Moses this assignment, he
had been a fugitive for 40 years (Moses made a knee jerk reaction, killing an
Egyptian slave owner for beating a Hebrew slave). Moses begins Exodus 4 with
an honest dialogue with God saying, "suppose they will not believe me or listen

to my voice?" (Exod. 4:1) Beyond having the confidence to address Pharaoh, he confessed to God that he struggled massively with speech challenges. Perhaps it was a stutter or simply a lack of eloquence when Moses communicated. Whatever the communication blooper was, Moses knew he certainly was not equipped to serve God in a way that required speaking to a person of authority.

The story documenting the speech challenges of Moses reminds us of the dangers of focusing on our weaknesses rather than God's power. Moses was given a direct command by God and his job was to simply obey. God's job was to do everything else. Moses knew he was given a difficult assignment. However, he let his insecurities overshadow the joy of realizing that God called Moses to this honorable task. It is important to note that Moses offered excuse after excuse of why he was not the right guy for the job. But God refused the excuses, promised He would be with Moses every step of the way, and equipped him for this task.

God's reply to Moses beginning in Exodus 4:11 is a powerful example for all of us who craft excuses for why we are unable to obey God. God said, "Who has made man's mouth? Or who makes the mute, the deaf, the seeing, or the blind? Have not I, the Lord? Now therefore, go, and I will be with your mouth and teach you what you shall say." God chose Moses to reflect His glory to the world, just as He chose you to follow through with the calling He has placed in your life. If He has called you, He will equip you! Paul's words to the Thessalonians echo this sentiment when he writes, "He who calls you is faithful, who also will do it" (1 Thess. 5:24). This verse comes to mind almost daily when I struggle to have the confidence to finish a project that God called me to start (this book!) Paul writes these words to remind us that the Lord will sanctify you completely as you allow Him to transform you inside and out.

Lord, I ask You to completely equip me with a fresh confidence to do the work You have called me to. Allow me to not focus on my weaknesses, but rather on the Holy Spirit's power to do the things You have ordained for me. Help me remember that if God has called me, He will equip me with what I need, according to His purposes. Amen.

-》》》》)《《《《-

God Equips His People
To Become a New Creation

Therefore, if anyone is in Christ, he is a new creation; old things have passed away; behold, all things have become new.
—*2 CORINTHIANS 5:17*

The phrase "sins of the father" originated from the Bible. Several Old Testament books including Exodus, Numbers, Deuteronomy, and Jeremiah cover this topic. Even Shakespeare touches on this topic in *The Merchant of Venice* saying, "the sins of the father are to be laid upon children." Current popular culture suggests this literary theme is still found in books, movies, and music.

God intended His people to understand that the actions of the parents will indeed impact descendants. He desired His people to understand the full impact of their sin and know that sin has consequences for future generations.

We cannot live in opposition to God's commandments and expect no adverse effects of sin. The Bible teaches that those unfortunate consequences of sin are transmitted through generations. However, in Christ Jesus *we have hope!* He is the ultimate chain breaker for generational sins. The 2020 film *Selfie Dad* delivered a solid message about breaking the cycle of generational sin, by the power of the cross. The movie was scheduled for a theatrical release, but the chaos of the world during that time allowed for only a video-on-demand release. The movie is excellent and describes the life of a dad in mid-life crisis. He was a former stand-up comic, who transitioned to a career as a social media star. During that journey, he experiences a radical shift in perspective and becomes aware that God can equip him to break the cycle of generational sin in his life.

The righteousness of Christ fills a life that we cannot live apart from Him. No matter how hard we try and no matter what efforts we make, we are unable to live the sin free life that was modeled by Jesus because of the broken world we know. Trusting in Him, we can overcome the battle of generational sin and model a life of righteousness for the next generation. For born again believers of Jesus, this means we share a divine nature (see John 3:3, 1 Pet. 1:23, and 2 Pet. 1:4). Our new identity is tied to our new birth (see Astounding Truth #14), and therefore, we are called to live in accordance with our new identity in Christ.

Paul wrote these words on becoming a new creation in Christ to the people of Corinth to ultimately summarize our experience of redemption. He wanted the Corinthians to understand what God did when He sent His son Jesus to die on the cross to save them from their sin. God's people are chosen (Eph. 1:4), justified (Rom. 8:1), sanctified (1 Cor. 1:2) and glorified in Christ (John 17:4–5). These words help us meditate on the significance of our union with Jesus. Knowing that God has equipped His people to be fully redeemed should bring us perfect peace (see Ps. 111:9, which states "Holy and awesome is His name").

Lord, equip me with Your knowledge and confidence that by Your Son Jesus, I am a completely different creation. I aim to be more like You, and less like me. Change my sinful ways and allow me to be bold with my testimony of what You have done in my life, by the death and Resurrection of Your son Jesus. Amen.

-﹥﹥﹥﹥﹤﹤﹤﹤﹤-

God Equips Us To Know That No Sin Is Greater Than the Cross

For son dishonors father, Daughter rises against mother, Daughter-in-law against mother-in-law; A man's enemies are the men of his own household. Therefore I will look to the Lord; I will wait for the God of my salvation; My God will hear me.

—MICAH 7:6–7

Micah is known as a minor prophet, yet nothing was minor about the message he was called to deliver to expose sin and share the message of salvation through Christ. Micah offers a buffet of literary forms throughout his short book including lament, prayer, and praise. However, his dominant writing style is scathing judgment speeches intended to hype the reader into a harsh realization of their shortcomings and awaken them toward an attitude of repentance (thank you Micah—I receive it!) Micah is also God's poster boy for speaking justice for the poor, oppressed, and downtrodden of society. The Astounding Truth that we learn from Micah is found in the final verses of his book—that regardless of how nasty our sin is, no sin is too great for the power of the cross.

The seventh and final chapter of the book of Micah begins with an unleashing of complaints. Micah calls it precisely as he sees it—no one is righteous anymore. Unjust leaders take bribes; friends betray friends; the rich take advantage of the lower class; and families are downright dysfunctional (Mic. 7:6). As if that list is not enough to blow your mind, Micah drops a bomb in the next verse. Verse 7 says "Therefore I will look to the Lord; I will wait for the God of my salvation; My God will hear me." Micah knows that regardless of the brokenness of his peers, he is steadfast in his awareness that God has a plan to make things right.

Micah lands the plane with a powerful praise and reminder of what God did for us by sending his son Jesus to die for us. Through Jesus, we can expect our sins to be as if they are cast into the depths of the sea (Mic. 7:19). Jesus went to the cross to pardon our sin. Without Jesus we are eternally separated from God. However, because of Him, we have a place in heaven waiting for us. That is a spectacular blessing we receive when we invite Jesus to be the Lord of our life and realize that our sin can be cast into the depths of the sea.

No sin is too great for the power of the cross. Nothing we have done is beyond God's redemptive work in our lives. This is especially encouraging to remember when it is challenging to forget a sinful past. Today we can receive mercy and grace in place of our guilt and shame (AMEN!) Because of the work on the cross, we can also extend mercy and grace to others because of what we know God has done for us.

Lord, I ask today that you set me free from my guilt of past sin. Because of Your work on the cross, I no longer need to dwell in shame. Thank You for Your grace and mercy. Thank You for washing me clean and sending my sin to the bottom of the sea. Help me receive Your love today. Amen.

God Equips Us With Wisdom

If any of you lacks wisdom, let him ask of God, who gives to all liberally and without reproach, and it will be given to him.

—*JAMES 1:5*

The topic of biblical wisdom triggers a joyful memory of my daughter, Lucy, when she was a cute kindergartner wearing glasses and pigtails. Her first assigned memory verse was on wisdom, so I helped her commit James 1:5 to memory. My assistance was marginal, however, because when she stood before her class to recite the verse beginning with "If any of you lacks wisdom…" she said instead, "If any of you *blacks* wisdom, let him ask of God, who gives liberally and without reproach, and it will be given to him." Her teacher was gracious, and lovingly assisted in redirecting her to the truth of the Word. Nevertheless, the message was understood. Lacking wisdom can be solved with a simple solution—just ask!

James opens his book with a powerful reminder for all of us who struggle with knowing what to do or what to say. James tells us to ask God for wisdom, and He will give liberally and without reproach. This means He will not scold, criticize, or roast you for a heartfelt request, admitting that you need help discerning how to proceed in life.

The writer of the book of James is most likely the brother of Jesus, who ironically was not a follower of Jesus during his earthly ministry. By the grace of God, the power of the Resurrection led James to saving faith. The writing style of this book is bold. James wants us to know if we are going to do this Christian life, we should not play around. The short book offers practical advice on everyday life. Within the first several verses of his book, James reminds us how to act when we come to a fork in the road.

This book opens with a bold statement: "count it all joy when you fall into various trials" (James 1:2). What do you do when trouble begins? *Pray*. What do you do when you have a difficult conversation in your future? *Pray*. When you are challenged in a close relationship…*pray*. When life's circumstances are beyond understanding…*pray*. When you are hurt by someone and do not know how to appropriately respond…*pray*. Ask God for wisdom, just as King Solomon did when he was presented with challenges. God promises to give you wisdom to respond to your trials because He equips us with it when we submit our needs to Him.

Lord, when I am uncertain on how to proceed, I humbly ask for Your wisdom. Please guide me, lead me, and direct my thoughts to be aware of Your presence in my life. Help me remember to lean on You in seasons of difficulty. Give me a desire to submit all my decisions to you. Amen.

-⟩⟩⟩⟩⟩❬❬❬❬❬-

God Equips His People with Discernment in Choosing Friends

The words of his mouth were smoother than butter, But war was in his heart; His words were softer than oil, Yet they were drawn swords.
—*PSALM 55:21*

Smooth like butter became a catchy lyric when the Korean Boy Band known as BTS sang a hit song that opened with these words. The song was praised by critics for its catchiness. It has a great beat and is easy for people like me who cannot carry a tune to sing along. Who knew butter could be such a tasty topic for these pop stars to sing about, but the song made music history with chart topping success in 2021 and aided in the band bringing billions of dollars to the South Korean economy. However, these K-pop boys were not the first to use this idiomatic expression and put the spotlight on the satisfying images of butter being smoothed over your favorite carbs.

Smooth like butter was a phrase that was uttered by King David as a poetic way of expressing anguish when he realized he was deceived by his frenemy, Ahithophel. The word "frenemy" was added to the Oxford English Dictionary in 2008 due to a rise in popularity. It means a person with whom one is friendly despite a fundamental dislike or rivalry. In essence, King David's friend broke an agreement with him. This action does not go unnoticed by God.

King David thought he and his closest friend were *butter* together, but when David discovered he had been betrayed by his top advisor, Ahithophel, news spread like warm butter on a hot roll. David reveals his true feelings of distress in Psalm 55:21 saying, "The words of his mouth were smoother than butter, but war was in his heart." The war David writes of was the desire his friend had to take the throne away from David. His plan was to pick out 12,000 men and go after David when he was exhausted and take him by surprise (see 2 Sam. 15). By God's grace, the revolt failed. Knowing his days were numbered, Ahithophel got his affairs in order and took his own life (2 Sam. 17:23).

The butter metaphor for betrayal reminds us to be wise and discerning in deciding who we share our carbs with. David laments "Even my close friend, someone I trusted, one who shared my bread, has turned against me." (Ps. 41:9) Jesus himself dealt with a nasty betrayal from Judas, one of the disciples who ironically also took his own life after realizing the grievous effects of his choices. The devil himself seeks to deceive and betray us into thinking that allegiance to him will lead to a life of abundance. The Lord is sovereignly in control of all our relationships. God chooses to raise leaders into power. God also chooses who will experience the challenge of having a door closed when success is not part of God's plan. We learn from the story of Ahithophel that God chose to spare David's life in order to accomplish His will for His people.

Lord, help me be discerning in choosing friendships. Bless me with friendships that are Christ-centered and will aid in kingdom building. Allow my relationships with my peers to be for Your glory. Give me clarity of mind to avoid friendships that will pull me away from You and lead me into temptation. You are sovereign over all my relationships. Thank you Lord! Amen.

-->>>>>><<<<<-

God Equips His People to Have a Winning Attitude At Work

Work willingly at whatever you do, as though you were working for the Lord rather than for people.

—*COLOSSIANS 3:23, NLT*

The movie *Horrible Bosses* is a dark comedy that shares the story of three friends who are manipulated by their respective supervisors and conspire to murder their dreadful bosses. The storyline of this 2001 film is hardly unique. Long before Jennifer Aniston, Colin Ferrell, and Kevin Spacey starred as horrible bosses, the Bible describes a horrendous boss who used cunning maneuvers to scheme his way into the bad boss hall of fame. The aforementioned story is found in Genesis 29, and it is certainly difficult to process how horrendous this biblical bad boss was. However, the astounding truth we can glean from Scripture is a message of hope for those of us who have struggled with a winning attitude in the workplace.

Paul tells the new covenant believers to *work as if they are working for the Lord, not for men.* With a kingdom mindset regarding work, we are instructed by God to produce excellence for His glory. We see this message about work modeled in the Old Testament in a story about Jacob. In a divine appointment, Jacob meets Rachel (Gen. 29:10–11) and Scripture records that upon meeting her, he had a complete emotional meltdown after and kissed her. From the context clues provided by the author Moses, we can gather that it was love at first sight. Rachel was beautiful in form and appearance (Gen. 29:17). An agreement was arranged for Jacob to have Rachel as his wife. He would work seven years for her father Laban in exchange for his daughter's hand in marriage. Scripture tells us that those seven years felt like only a few days because he loved Rachel so much (Gen. 29:20). Those words may be the loveliest words ever penned about a man's feelings for a woman.

At the time of the wedding celebration, Laban put a veil on his older daughter, Leah, (not as pretty as her sister) and sent her down the aisle. Unfamiliar with Laban's scheming and manipulative ways, Jacob was completely dumbstruck the next morning to discover that he had married Rachel's older sister, Leah. Nevertheless, his love for Rachel was unrelenting. He was expected to work another seven years to have Rachel as his wife. Even though this was unfair, Jacob was a loyal and patient employee because he knew that was what God expected of him.

As a result of Laban's tricks, Jacob ended up with two wives, and eventually two concubines. Laban also displayed his deceitful nature by removing animals from the flocks he had promised to Jacob. From Laban's example, we get an understanding of how wrong it is to manipulate people. It is dishonest and selfish. Yet, God sees the sinful ways of those who work to manipulate situations to get what they want. The story of Jacob and his love triangle serves as a reminder that God is sovereign throughout the chaos and sin of broken people like Laban. God worked through this family and used the marital relationships of this sister switcheroo to make up the twelve tribes of Israel.

Lord, grant me Your grace to carry me through difficult times at my workplace. Give me Your favor with my employers and allow me to have a Colossians 3:23 attitude at my workplace. Allow me opportunities to show Your love to others who do not know You at my workplace. Amen.

-»»»»«««-

God Equips People to Recognize Miracles

Suddenly there was a great earthquake, so that the foundations of the prison were shaken; and immediately all the doors were opened and everyone's chains were loosed.

—*ACTS 16:26*

Hardships. Suffering. Affliction. Misery. Distress. Whatever you call hard times, no one is immune to them. It is something every human will endure on this side of the cross. In my flesh, I deal with adversity by consuming copious amounts of hard salami, cheese, and dark chocolate. Ten out of ten would not recommend this strategy. The Bible provides an alternative solution when dealing with challenging times. It's a much better solution and will not leave you with processed food gas pains.

Knowing the Bible and what the major players of Scripture endured to lead others to the faith can encourage us in our testimony to be bold and have persistence when dealing with hardships. The Bible records many challenges the apostle Paul faced throughout his ministry. Acts 16:16 begins the story of when Paul and his friend Silas were thrown into jail for coming to the aid of a young girl who endured trials (she experienced the modern equivalent of human trafficking). She was a slave, possessed by demons, and made her owners rich by fortune telling. The Bible contains over one hundred verses about staying clear of anything that has an association with sorcery, omens, and mediums, and calls them *abdominal practices*. Scripture tells us that Paul was greatly "anroyed" (Acts 16:18) by the publicity that this nonsense received and commanded the demons to leave her young body. He prayed in the name of Jesus and as a result the demons obeyed and miraculously she was healed.

Once the slave masters realized their hope for big profits was no longer possible, they dragged Paul and Silas to the authorities. The magistrate tore off their clothes, commanded them to be beaten, and threw them into jail.

The supernatural events did not cease once the prison doors were locked. As a result of Paul's prayers and praises to God, the Philippian jail master underwent a radical heart transplant (see Astounding Truth #64) and asked how he could obtain salvation. Paul's testimony to remain steadfast through his imprisonment led the jailer *and* his family to believe in Christ and be baptized (Acts 16:33). This event also led Paul to Thessalonica where he continued to effect change in the lives of many followers of Christ. God will use your trials, challenges, and dark times to relentlessly pursue you and lovingly make His kingdom available to ALL who choose to open their heart to His ways. Like Paul, your testimony of hardship can be used as a model of faith to the lost. This offers so much encouragement to the believer in a season of storms. Like Paul, remain prayerful through trials, and let God do the miraculous work only He can do in the lives of His people.

Lord, equip me with Your peace when I journey through seasons of hardship. Help me remain faithful to Your promises and aware that kingdom work can occur during difficult seasons. By the power of Your Holy Spirit, redirect the sinful ways of people who do not know Your presence in their lives. Amen.

-›››››‹‹‹‹-

God Equips Us for Unexpected Plans

Abraham and Sarah were both very old by this time, and Sarah was
long past the age of having children. So she laughed silently to herself
and said, "How could a worn-out woman like me enjoy such pleasure,
especially when my master—my husband—is also so old?"
—GENESIS 18:11–12, NLT

"We plan, God laughs." This proverbial truth is probably something we all can relate to when circumstances do not fall in line with the outcome we expect. Maybe you completed your education at a university you didn't expect to enroll in. Maybe you land in a career you didn't expect to work in. Maybe you married the person you didn't expect to marry. Maybe you had more (or less) kids than you expected. The concept of us making plans and God laughing is found in the book of *Not Biblical 24:7*. The Biblical truth is that God is always sovereign over our plans. We see this in Genesis 18. The text confirms that sometimes the Lord's plans are not what we may have orchestrated for ourselves, and sometimes the one laughing is us—not God.

This was the case of Abraham and his wife, Sarah, when they laughed upon hearing God's plan for their family. The text describes Sarah eavesdropping when she heard God tell Abraham that she would have a son and scoffed behind the tent door. She could not believe the absurdity of having a baby at her age. Apparently, her husband had failed to pass along the critical lesson he learned when he laughed at God (Gen. 17:3). Abraham was one hundred years old, and Sarah was ninety when their son was born, and the baby was appropriately named Isaac (meaning *he laughs*).

Abraham and Sarah serve as poster children for doubting God and His providence. In Genesis 18 we see Abraham was faithful and obeyed God's promises, even when they were not easy and seemed humorous. They trusted God in His timing when God said they would have a baby, even though they waited years to see the fulfillment of that promise. Despite her original skepticism and ridicule, Sarah eventually joined her husband and came to believe the promise God had spoken over Abraham to be the father of the great and powerful nation of Israel. God was faithful in His timing and made a way through this couple of advanced age to fulfill His promise and His plans.

Lord, open my eyes to Your redemptive plan over my life. Deliver me from comfort and complacency and purge me from the temptation to listen to other voices over Your voice. Help me first seek You for discernment over my plans. Thank you for leading me and directing my path. Amen.

-》》》》《《《《-

God Equips Us To Be Part of a Royal Priesthood

But you are a chosen generation, a royal priesthood, a holy nation,
His own special people, that you may proclaim the praises of Him who
called you out of darkness into His marvelous light.

—*1 PETER 2:9*

The Halloween costumes in our home rotate on a four-year schedule. This is not a rigid schedule per se; flexibility is granted based on weather conditions and current moods. My family has fun with this pagan holiday, knowing it is a great day for evangelism and sharing the Good News of Christ with our neighbors and friends. Some years, my entire family has participated in the theme (we've been a family of crayons and a family of superheroes), while other years only Mr. and Mrs. Weber participate in the themed costume festivities. The couple theme which has attracted the most attention has been the priest and nun duds.

The Bible teaches about being part of a royal priesthood (1 Pet. 2:9). However, this priesthood that St. Peter described is not the priesthood you may be inclined to imagine. Images of a man wearing a white collar and black cassock may come to mind when you think of a priest. Peter is speaking of the priesthood that God originally identified to serve as a bridge between people who worship idols and people who would eventually come to believe in God. God told his people that they were a kingdom of priests. That is precisely what Peter is calling followers of Jesus. His intent was to remind the early Christians of the duties of priests—they intercede for people before God; they shepherd God's people; they guide people to the One True God; and they teach the Word of God.

While my husband, Bryan, does not identify as a the type of priest we think of today—a black robe topped with a white clergy collar—he is absolutely a priest in the biblical sense. He is called to show the love of Christ to his family and the people God has called into his life. He is called to teach and share the Word of God. He is called to live a life that honors God. Every person who is a follower of Christ has the same calling over their life.

Peter's description of the royal priesthood reminds us that through Jesus, we have direct access to God. This is called the *priesthood of the believer* and was not the case before Jesus came to earth. Under the Old Testament Law, very few priests held the honor of coming into God's presence. The priests were called to represent humans before God because regular people were unworthy to appear before God. However, today we need no other human priest to represent us or intercede for us. The death of Jesus put an end to the Old Testament Covenant and the Levitical priesthood (evidenced by the splitting of the temple veil, see Matt. 27:51).

Because of Jesus, we are all given an all-access pass directly to God. We have the full assurance of faith because of the sacrifice of Jesus. He made a way for us to approach God directly. We can come to God any day, any time, with any concerns. We can confess our sin and brokenness, and He will hear the cry of our hearts (see also Heb. 10:19–22 for more on the priesthood).

As if the news of having direct access to God is not enough to blow your mind, Peter also communicates in this text that followers of Jesus are also a holy nation. We are set apart for God's possession. Peter stresses the importance of Christians being special not because of who we are, but *whose* we are. He reminds us that unlike the people in the nation of Israel who were identified as God's people because of their bloodline and common homeland, new covenant believers (followers of Jesus) come from every nation and culture. This is great news for someone like me (and possibly you?) who was not born into the Jewish faith. The work of Jesus, coupled with my belief in Christ, secures a place for me to spend eternity with God—thank you Lord for this gift!

Lord, equip me to be bold in my calling as a priest. Give me the grace to live in abundance because I am part of a Holy Nation. Allow the words of St. Peter to guide my thoughts regarding my role as part of a royal priesthood. Thank You for the ability to come directly to You for repentance. Amen.

God Equips Us For Miraculous Healing

Then they brought to Him one who was deaf and had an impediment in his speech, and they begged Him to put His hand on him.

—MARK 7:32

A lbert Einstein is best known for his crazy hair and his famous equation that energy and matter are related. He was a physicist and mathematician. His work led to understanding the theory of relativity, photoelectric effect, and a slew of other scientific terms that are way above my pay grade. Beyond his scientific work, Einstein also had a philosophical side. He once quoted, "There are only two ways to live your life. One is as though nothing is a miracle. The other is as though everything is a miracle."[5]

The Bible also has much to say on miracles. One of my favorite Biblical miracles described in Mark 7 is a stark reminder of the testimony of how the Lord Jesus has healed me. The text describes a man who suffered two disabilities being brought to Jesus. Due to rising popularity and the reputation Jesus had among the Gentiles for performing astounding miracles, the deaf and mute man was brought before Jesus to be healed. Mark 7:31 tells us the events took place in a region called Decapolis (Greek word for "Ten Towns"). Jesus was

---

5 Quotes.net, STANDS4 LLC, 2023. "Albert Einstein Quotes." Accessed August 18, 2023. https://www.quotes.net/quote/9350.

intentionally visiting cities outside the nation of Israel to model to His followers that the message He came to share was for the God-fearing Jews *and* Gentiles.

This text serves as a personal invitation to rejoice in the fact that Jesus came for you, even if you live outside the designated land He intended for His people. He is gracious to let the Good News expand beyond the nation of Israel located in the Middle East to places like the Decapolis (and Guam, or Michigan or wherever you are currently reading this).

The disabilities this man had were severe. He lived his entire life unable to hear and speak. That meant his only options for survival included a life of begging. While this scenario may not be familiar to you if you have hearing and speech capabilities, his disabilities illustrate the spiritual disabilities that you may be familiar with. While you may not be deaf, you may have had seasons of spiritual hearing impairments which did not allow you to hear the voice of God. The metaphor of this miracle forces us to remember that we must have ears to hear the Truth of God.

Upon learning about the disabilities this man suffered, Jesus took him aside, put His fingers in the man's ears, and spit on the man's tongue (Mark 7:33). Stay with me here, because I know that just got weird. Even the saliva of the Son of God was used for His glory (see John 9:6). The actions of Jesus did not fall in line with the etiquette that honored social distance, but He did not care. Jesus touched the man in the places where he was broken, just as He can heal you where you are broken. Jesus knew what the man needed to be healed. He also knows what you need to be healed. Trust that if you are willing to let Him change you, He will provide a solution for the impossible.

Lord, thank You for the reminder from Mark 7 that Jesus cares about those who are social outcasts. He knows everyone and knows how to heal our spiritual ailments and disabilities as part of His sovereign plan. God, please touch me in places where You know I need a spiritual, emotional, and physical healing. Amen.

God Equips Us for Meetings in Obscure Places

And I give them eternal life, and they shall never perish; neither shall anyone snatch them out of My hand. My Father, who has given them to Me, is greater than all; and no one is able to snatch them out of My Father's hand. I and My Father are one.

—*JOHN 10:28–30*

Sometimes God allows the most unsuspecting mission work to be done in the most obscure places. Not everyone hears the Good News of Christ and has a true heart transformation in a church environment, a Bible study, a campus ministry, a youth group, a Vacation Bible School, or any other setting that has been purposely created for people to grow close to Christ. I've met people who have met the Lord in prison. I've also met people who were exposed to faith in their workplace because a coworker was unfiltered about the Lord's work in their life. The Holy Spirit never ceases to amaze me. He is astounding and He can open the eyes of the unbeliever in the most unsuspecting places.

We see this in Scripture modeled by Jesus when He had yet another conversation with the "religious elite" of His time. The Jewish people—God's chosen people—were celebrating an eight-day celebration at Solomon's Colonnade (a fancy word for porch). The environment was certainly an atmosphere where the religious leaders could have believed the message that Jesus was trying to tell them—that He was God in the flesh, that He was sent to enlighten His people, and give them eternal life (John 10:28). However, the message fell on deaf ears. The Israelites refused to believe the message Jesus came to proclaim. They asked for Jesus to "tell them plainly" (John 10:24), but the truth hurt. The Jews responded in a completely appropriate way; a way you might expect grown men to respond. They picked up rocks to throw at Jesus (see John 10:31).

After another failed attempt to silence him, Scripture tells us that Jesus escaped from the temple. He left Jerusalem and retreated to the Jordanian wilderness. It was in that location where the Holy Spirit did His best conversion work of the day. The wilderness is where *many* people believed in Him (John 10:42).

Unlike the Jewish people who were lifelong students committed to the study of God and were considered religious scholars, these people He met in the wilderness completely recognized the miracles they had witnessed. They realized that these miracles were the fulfillment of prophecy that God would send a Messiah to offer His people salvation. The wilderness proved to be an unexpected location where many people believed the Gospel for the first time.

Lord, Your transformational power knows no locational limits. Meet me in obscure places and draw me closer to You. Allow me to remember that salvation is not dependent on my grip on You, rather Your grip on me. Meet me where I am today because I know I can't do life without You. I know You have promised to save those who turn from sin and put their faith in You. Today I trust You to forgive my past and give me eternal life. Thank You for dying in my place to make salvation possible. Amen.

L ike the Jewish people celebrating, I met the Lord in a season of wilderness. I love the wilderness, and taking long treks through public land that is uncultivated is lifegiving for me (as long as the ticks decide to remain in nature.) However, biblical wilderness does not warrant that same reaction from me. Biblical wilderness represents isolation and hardship—No. Thank. You —I am not excited to partake in *that* wilderness experience.

Since Adam and Eve disobeyed God by eating the fruit they were told not to eat, the fellowship they had with God was broken. As a result, sin entered the world. Sin is a disease far more deadly than any pandemic we could experience. Everyone is affected by this condition. Sin is more terminal than any virus or pox because it leads to eternal death.

The perfect experience God intended for humans was thwarted when sin entered the world. Because of that choice, every human experiences pain and hardship. The agony of life's trials, strained relationships, unforgiveness, and tribulations are sometimes so overwhelming that all we can do is cry out and say *why me*? These things are not evidence that God does not care for you; they are products of a fallen world. Read that previous sentence again and say it louder for the people in the back.

However, God chose not to let us remain in this wilderness forever. He provided a plan for us to have hope and to live the life he intended us to live, in close relationship with Him. Whatever wilderness you are currently experiencing, God has you. God loves you. God desires you to feel His peace and know that there is good news. We know that while every disease does not have a cure, there is a cure for sin. God sent His one and only Son to die for every person so we could have that perfect relationship with him. All you need to do is admit your need, turn away from sin, and believe that Jesus died for you.

With that, I end Section IV with only one reflective question:

Do you choose to accept Jesus as your personal Lord and savior?

If you say Yes, I want to know! Please reach out so I can celebrate with you and share in the joy that we will be together for eternity with the Lord Jesus. Thank you for joining me in this journey through Astounding Truths. May God bless you for your faithfulness to study His word and develop a more intimate relationship with Him!

ACKNOWLEDGEMENTS AND GRATITUDE TO MY FAMILIES

To my ministry family:

The ministry of Community Bible Study has been transformative in my understanding of the Bible. Serving as a leader in this ministry has equipped me with the confidence and love to wash feet of all sizes. Thank you CBS for equipping me to have a solid understanding of God's word and thank you to everyone I have served in leadership alongside.

To my publishing family:

I am so thankful for the vision of Brian Dixon, founder of hope*books. I am thankful for the encouragement and servant leadership of director Krissy Nelson, and her knowledge of the publishing business. I am grateful to my awesome development editor, TJ Ray for his wisdom, insights, and patience with my ridiculous spelling and grammatical errors. I am thankful for the friendships and support of the other authors with whom I share this journey. May God bless your ministries and continue to give you a love for Him and His people.

To my church family:

I am in awe of the faithful community affiliated with Harvest Ministries in Barrigada, Guam. Thank you to my pastors, deacons, leaders, and church family for the way you care and minister to our island community. I am blessed to be part of such an amazing church and blessed by your friendship.

To my blood family—Mom, Dad, Julie, and Christie:

You all were an intricate part of my faith formation. It was in my childhood home where I learned the tenets of the faith. I am extremely grateful for you all and our time together. May God bless you and deepen your love for Him. Thank you for serving as my cheerleaders during the creative process of writing this book. I love you!

www.ingramcontent.com/pod-product-compliance
Lightning Source LLC
Chambersburg PA
CBHW071155130626
46553CB00004B/1666